I Have a Plan

I Have a Plan

A Pastor's Guide to Counseling
Troubled Marriages

Charles L. Rassieur

WESTMINSTER
JOHN KNOX PRESS
LOUISVILLE • KENTUCKY

Book design by Sharon Adams
Cover design by Eric Walljasper, Minneapolis, MN

First edition
Published by Westminster John Knox Press
Louisville, Kentucky

This book is printed on acid-free paper that meets the American National Standards Institute Z39.48 standard. ♾

PRINTED IN THE UNITED STATES OF AMERICA

05 06 07 08 09 10 11 12 13 14 — 10 9 8 7 6 5 4 3 2 1

Library of Congress Cataloging-in-Publication Data is on file at the Library of Congress, Washington, D.C.

ISBN 0-664-22762-7

To parish pastors,
for whom I have the highest regard and respect,
and most particularly to those who share my passion
for the church's ministry to couples and families

Contents

Preface

The origin of this book and its earlier version can best be traced to a telephone call I received in 1985 from Professor William Smith at Luther Northwestern Theological Seminary, now Luther Seminary, in St. Paul. At that time I had been a professional marriage counselor, besides also counseling with individuals and families, for thirteen years. In addition to being a pastoral counselor I was also a licensed psychologist. Professor Smith presented me with a challenge. He explained that he and Dr. Roland Martinson were teaching a course for seniors about family care, and that the students had been clearly told in the course that marriage counseling was beyond their expertise and that they should not attempt it in the parish. "Chuck," Professor Smith put his invitation to me, "would you consider doing a workshop with our seniors to show them what they *can* do as pastors to intervene responsibly when they learn of a conflicted marriage in their church?"

I gladly accepted Professor Smith's invitation because by this time I had developed my own method and practice for working with couples and decided that I could tailor my clinical method to fit with the realistic constraints of the limited time and professional expertise of parish pastors. That short-term model designed specifically for pastors was the subject matter of the workshop requested by Professor Smith, and was further developed in my book, *Pastor, Our Marriage Is in Trouble: A Guide to Short-Term Counseling* (Westminster Press, 1988).

Since Professor Smith's initial invitation, I was regularly invited by Dr. Martinson to present this short-term model to seniors at Luther Seminary until the spring of 2001. Then I wrote to nearly four hundred of those students, now pastors, to request their feedback about the short-term pastoral marriage counseling model. The following reply from one of the pastors helped confirm my decision that a new, revised book would once again be a valuable resource for parish clergy:

> Dr. Rassieur, thank you so much for this resource and for coming to our class all those years ago. Know that you have provided an excellent resource for at least one pastor. Seminary doesn't provide much in terms of practical tools for ministry, but your system sure has helped me to help struggling couples.

New features in this revised edition include summaries at the beginning of each chapter, new counseling vignettes and cases, summaries of the counseling process, an initial covenant for counseling, a revised counseling questionnaire, four resources to aid pastors, and Internet references in the notes for the reader's easy access. My intention has been to make each chapter more "user friendly," particularly for the pastor who does not very often do couple counseling and who will be helped by a reliable plan when a troubled marriage comes to his or her attention.

Some parts of the first book remain as relevant and appropriate as they originally were, and therefore have been retained in this revised edition. Of course, the basic short-term marriage counseling model itself remains unchanged, but much of this revised edition contains new material for the presentation and explanation of that model. As a matter of style, the inclusions from the first book have not been noted.

Chapter 1 discusses theoretical and theological considerations for understanding marriage and intervening in troubled marriages with a hopeful pastoral counseling dialogue. The outline of the short-term plan is also introduced. Chapter 2 explains how the marriage counseling plan is implemented with the pastor's invitation and initial meeting with the couple. In this chapter two essential instruments are presented, the Covenant for Pastoral Marriage Counseling and the Pastoral Marriage Counseling Questionnaire. In chapter 3 the focus is on the plan for the pastor meeting individually with each of the spouses. Detailed attention is given to the Pastoral Marriage Counseling Questionnaire, which is found in appendix B. The final two sessions with the couple are discussed in chapter 4, including consideration of the pastor's three counseling options after assessing with the couple the progress made so far. Those options include recommending the termination of the counseling, referring to another professional counseling resource, or contracting for a maximum of three more joint counseling sessions with the pastor. Chapter 5 reviews critical issues that may very well be encountered by the counseling pastor. Several references are made in the notes to Internet sites. Those sites were all current as of June 1, 2005.

The reader will find fictional narratives and counseling vignettes to help pastors understand how best to recognize and respond to conflicted couples in their congregation. In many instances the descriptions are composites of typical parish counseling situations that do not describe any single or particular couple. In descriptions of actual counselees or marriages, the unique, identifying features of the individuals have been omitted so persons and circumstances are not recognizable. Any apparent similarities of cases in the following pages to actual persons or circumstances are coincidental.

I am particularly thankful to Dr. Roland Martinson for his enthusiastic support of this marriage counseling model as he invited me year after year to present this model to the seniors at Luther Seminary. His thoughtful and encouraging insights have always been very helpful.

I also wish to express my gratitude to my friend William D. Tallevast, who years ago introduced me to the Biographical Marital Questionnaire published in Bernard L. Greene's book, *A Clinical Approach to Marital Problems: Evaluation and Management* (1970). Greene's questionnaire convinced me of the many benefits of using a questionnaire in the earliest stages of the marriage counseling process. The one presented in this book is very similar to the questionnaire I used for many years in my counseling work with couples. Clergy are invited to reproduce and use the Pastoral Marriage Counseling Questionnaire for their work with couples.

I owe a debt of gratitude to several of my colleagues over the years in different staff settings as well as the professional consultants who were available to us. They have all been my valued teachers in the art of pastoral counseling. To name them all would make a long list, and I would be afraid of leaving someone out. Suffice it to say, I am very thankful for how they helped shape me as a counselor, and thus contributed importantly to this book for pastors.

Four friends willingly accepted my invitation to read the preliminary draft of this book, two women and two men, two parish pastors and two professional psychologists: the Rev. Daniel Rondeau, the Rev. Karen Siegfriedt, Dr. Joan Duke, and Dr. Richard Friberg. They are each highly regarded professional persons, and I am very grateful for the time they gave to this project and for their invaluable and insightful observations.

I also want to acknowledge with much gratitude the generous assistance and guidance of Betty Clements, reference librarian at the Claremont School of Theology. Likewise, my thanks go to her colleague, Elaine Walker, the circulation librarian, for her courtesy and the kind consideration she extended to me. My heartfelt thanks also go to our neighbor, Frances Tillis, who carefully read the copyedited draft and the page proofs and offered many helpful recommendations. I am very appreciative that Jerri Rodewald responded so promptly to be a consulting reader. I gratefully remember, too, Dr. Bean Robinson, a professional psychologist and friend who responded to my repeated requests for bibliographical resources. And thank you also to my friend David Burgdorf, director of Residential Day Treatment at the Betty Ford Center, for making the library of that facility available to me.

Every writer needs a supportive publisher and editorial staff. David Dobson initially recognized the promise in revising my earlier book on marriage counseling. Likewise Jon Berquist was very affirming of this project and facilitated the publishing process moving ahead of the original schedule. Julie Tonini has promptly responded to e-mail questions. To them and their unnamed colleagues who have been part of this publishing effort I am very grateful for their careful attention to seeing this book through to its successful publication.

Finally, I cannot adequately relate my indebtedness or my depth of loving gratitude for my wife, Virginia, and her contribution at several levels to this writing project. Without our nearly forty-five years of marriage I would hardly know much at all about the many shared joys and the deepening fulfillment—and the considerable challenges—of such a loving and intimate relationship. Furthermore, as a computer analyst by profession, she has several times during my work on this manuscript rescued me from annoying computer problems that I mostly brought on myself. With this book on marriage now completed, we both eagerly look forward to focusing even more energy and time on our own marriage.

As always, many persons have necessarily been involved in making this counseling resource available to parish pastors. Now, however, I gladly accept full responsibility for all that appears in the following pages. Despite the shortcomings and limitations that will be evident to readers, I trust that many pastors will find this book to be a reliable plan for them as they faithfully respond to the highly rewarding challenge of helping troubled couples.

Palm Desert, California

C.L.R.

I Have a Plan

Marriage and family enrichment and marriage crisis counseling are among the pastor's most important helping skills.
—Howard J. Clinebell, *Basic Types of Pastoral Care and Counseling: Resources for the Ministry of Healing and Growth*

This chapter covers:

~ An introduction of the counseling plan
~ Insights for understanding marriage
~ Ten vital signs for a fulfilling marriage
~ A hopeful dialogue

Before the long-range planning committee even met at 7:00 p.m., Pastor Barbara Cowan figured it would be a long meeting, at least until 10:00. She was right. She was turning off the lights and pulling the church door shut just as she looked at her watch and was dismayed to see that it was 10:40. Turning toward her car, she saw one of the committee members, Mary Nelson, walking toward the parking lot, too.

Pastor Cowan and Mary both commented on how late the hour was, but Mary added, "No need for me to rush home, anyway. Ron has started going to bed early and never waits up for me, even when I'm home from these church meetings by 9:00."

"What do you mean?" Pastor Cowan asked. Mary looked down for a moment as she considered how much to reveal to her pastor. "To tell the truth, Pastor, for a couple months now Ron has been finding every excuse he can to avoid being awake when I'm in bed. I think something must be wrong, but I can't get Ron to talk about it!"

A minister does not have to be a licensed marriage counselor to recognize that Mary and Ron very likely have some significant problems in their marriage. The depth of those problems is not evident. The details offered by Mary may very well reflect long-standing difficulties, or this may only be a temporary episode caused by a recent misunderstanding. All that Pastor Cowan knows at the moment is that there is significant distress in the Nelson marriage, and late at night in a parking lot is not the place to begin pastoral counseling.

Some pastors might just ignore the signs of trouble in the Nelson marriage, or they might seek to avoid any counseling involvement by immediately giving the couple the name of a marriage counselor. But there is a growing number of pastors who have a responsible pastoral plan, based on a structured, short-term model, for intervening when a troubled marriage comes to their attention. Pastors in this increasingly expanding group do not see themselves as specialists or trained marriage counselors, but they affirm the challenge and the responsibility they have to provide sensitive and hopeful pastoral counseling to couples who are in a relationship crisis. Pastor Barbara Cowan is one of those pastors, and she confidently responds in the parking lot to her parishioner: "Mary, I'm sorry to hear that there seems to be some tension between you and Ron. It's late right now, but *I have a plan*, and here's what I'd like you to do. I want you and Ron to come to my office so the three of us can talk together. But, so you can do that, I want you to find a chance tomorrow to tell Ron that you mentioned some of your concerns to me and that I said I thought it would be best for the three of us to sit down together and talk. Then in a couple days I'll call and talk to either you or Ron about setting up a time for the three of us to meet at church. At that time I can tell you both about my plan for how the two of you might make positive progress."

Pastor Cowan has a plan for intervening pastorally and responsibly in the marital situation that has come to her attention late in the evening after a long church meeting. It is no surprise that Pastor Cowan has just encountered another troubled marriage in view of the fact that the failure rate of first marriages may approach fifty percent.[1] Knowing that so many marriages are at risk, even among her own parishioners, Pastor Cowan had intentionally planned and was prepared for the chance meeting she just had with Mary Nelson. Pastor Cowan's plan is both pastoral and responsible for intervening in a marriage crisis within parish ministry, because the plan meets certain essential criteria.

1. *It is time limited.* There is hardly any pastor who is not constantly balancing demanding priorities in order to make the most of each day. Pastors do not have the time available to do extended counseling with couples. An effective pastoral counseling model with couples should be able to reach stated goals within five to seven sessions.[2]

2. *It is within the competence level of parish clergy.* There is an abundance of literature on theories of couple therapy, with which the professional counselor specializing in marriage therapy should be familiar.[3] But with few exceptions, parish clergy have no specialized training in marriage counseling. At the most, clergy may have had two or three courses in counseling during their seminary education and perhaps a quarter of Clinical Pastoral Education. Parish clergy have been trained to be generalists in all areas of parish ministry. A viable model for pastoral marriage intervention must assume the limited counseling training most pastors have received.

3. *It is amenable to referrals.* In some instances pastors may make premature referrals because of their own anxiety about offering even limited help to a couple. On the other hand, every counseling situation certainly carries with it the potential that a referral to another counselor is the best choice for the couple. A responsible pastoral model for counseling couples should always include the option of making a referral at any time in the counseling process.

4. *It provides for efficiency in gathering information.* The pastor needs to gather essential data about each spouse and about the relationship. In a short-term model, that information must be gathered quickly and efficiently from the outset of the process. Furthermore, the information gathering should not take an inordinate amount of time away from other aspects of the counseling.

5. *It can help to manage conflicted and reactive spouses.* Most conflicted couples are typically overreactive to each other. A husband and wife with marital problems may very likely feel defensive in the other's presence, and then communication can often degenerate, even in the presence of their pastor, into nonproductive arguing. In order to reach stated goals for the counseling, the effective pastoral counseling model must manage the counseling process in such a way that couple conflict or arguing is less likely to dominate the counseling sessions.

6. *It will empower the couple to work together toward mutual understanding*

and resolution. More often than not, when a wife and husband come to a marriage counselor their relationship has become to some degree adversarial. Typically, they feel they have to defend their own "turf," while directing blame to the other and fending off the accusations directed at them. A major turning point in productive marriage counseling occurs when a couple can move beyond an adversarial stance and take steps in a cooperative, covenant-based partnership approach toward the counseling process.

7. *It sets clear goals for the counseling outcome.* The effective pastoral counseling plan will offer a troubled couple specific goals to be accomplished by the end of the process. In other words, before the couple even begins the counseling the couple knows what will happen at the end of the process. It can be very reassuring to a troubled couple to hear a pastor offer a counseling plan with specific goals to be accomplished.

8. *It acknowledges the need to manage complex pastor/parishioner relationships.* The parish pastor's primary identity in any counseling process is that of pastor. Before, during, and after the counseling the pastor remains the couple's pastor, and the pastor of *each* of the spouses. The pastoral relationship is the context for the counseling. However, as professional counselors well know, particularly within extended-term counseling, the relationship between the counselor and the counselee can become confusing, sometimes to both the counselor and the counselee. The potential for such confusion must be monitored and needs to be held to a minimum in pastoral marriage counseling.

9. *It has a balanced focus on the marriage relationship and individual responsibility.* The effective pastoral marriage counseling model keeps the focus on the relationship between both spouses, while at the same time never losing sight of the responsibility each spouse has for his or her own behavior in the relationship. Through such a counseling model couples discover and affirm that they can work together to change their relationship, while also acknowledging that they can only change themselves—not their spouse.

10. *It is applicable to alternative committed couples.* The statistics from the 2000 census show that nearly one in every twelve households maintained by couples has an unmarried male-female couple.[4] "Living together" is such a common phenomenon today, most pastors have to decide whether their pastoral care will extend beyond the "traditionally married" to all the other committed couples in the parish or congregation.[5] Furthermore, there is an increasing number of parishes where gay couples are affirmed and welcomed. The effective pastoral marriage counseling model, as a

process for the assessment and resolution of relationship conflicts, will be applicable to all committed relationships.

11. *It is adaptable to a variety of theologies.* For a pastoral counseling model to be useful for a large number of parish clergy, it should be applicable in almost any theological setting. Whether pastors consider themselves to be conservative, liberal, or somewhere in the middle of the theological spectrum, the effective pastoral marriage counseling model should meet their need to be of the most assistance possible to a distressed couple.

Pastor Cowan's plan meets all of these criteria.

The Plan for Brief Pastoral Marriage Counseling
A structured five-step model, five to seven sessions, fifty to sixty minutes in length.

1. The invitation
2. The initial session with the couple
3. One or two individual sessions with each spouse
4. One session with both spouses
5. The final counseling session, resulting in one of three options:
   a. Termination of the counseling
   b. Referral to a professional community resource
   c. Recontracting with the pastor for a maximum of three more joint counseling sessions

In chapter 2 I will explain the counseling plan so that all parish pastors can join Pastor Cowan in saying to troubled couples, "I have a plan to offer you for how you might make positive progress."

Insights for a Pastoral Understanding of Marriage

A pastor will want to be familiar with the following key biblical passages that inform our understanding of marriage:

Genesis 2:18–25	1 Corinthians 7:1–40
Exodus 20:1–17 (Deuteronomy 5:6–21)	Ephesians 5:21–33
Malachi 2:13-16	Hebrews 13:4
Matthew 19:3–12 (Mark 10:2–12)	1 Peter 3:1–7

These Scripture references describe the unique relationship between a man and a woman in marriage. Likewise, these passages reflect Middle

Eastern cultures of more than two thousand years ago that were patriarchal in their structure. The man was the head of the house, or more likely the head of the tent, and his wife took her orders from him. That long-standing perspective of how households were to be ordered did not, however, prevent wives from exercising considerable power. Rebekah's manipulative scheming with her son Jacob is an early example of the effective behind-the-scenes power of the wife of a patriarch.

The New Testament, however, shows us how Christianity brought a dramatically new dimension to patriarchal, Mediterranean cultures. The self-giving, dying love of Jesus Christ became the model for the Christian life and, consequently, also the model for ordering how Christian husbands and wives are to relate to each other. Although a few might contend today that Christian marriage requires the supremacy of the man over the woman, that position is not easy to defend when the biblical record is examined closely. Noteworthy are the conclusions of Diana S. Richmond Garland and David E. Garland, writing as faculty members of Southern Baptist Theological Seminary:

> We conclude from our study of the biblical evidence that man and wife were created by God to be equal partners in marriage. A hierarchical relationship in which the husband rules is not the will of God but a distortion of the relationship between man and woman. Although the forced repression of wives into submissive roles in marriage became an almost universal custom and was the normative view in the first century, we find in the New Testament the winds of change. Husbands are to love their wives in the same way Christ demonstrated his love for his people. They are not to put themselves first but their wives first. Wives are to be honored by their husbands as co-heirs of God's grace and therefore equals. Wives and husbands mutually rule over each other's bodies. The principle that is to govern the marriage relationship of those in Christ is therefore to be mutuality and partnership under the lordship of Christ.[6]

Our Christian heritage is clear that marriage is preeminently to be a loving relationship of mutual respect and honor between equals. Philip Culbertson concurs that sharing power is an important way marriages reflect their Christian character. He adds, "Other ways include voluntary sacrifice (though I do not imply self-negation); reconciliation, particularly in generous acts of forgiveness and charity; hospitality of home and heart; respect for the dignity of each partner as a living image of God; and shared opportunities for home prayer, quiet meditation, and formal worship."[7] The Bible conveys essential wisdom for today's marriages. But beyond the biblical teachings for Christian marriage, pastors will be aided in their work with couples by giving attention to further insights into the complex dynamics that are characteristic of most contemporary marriages.

Today there is no shortage of theories and explanations for how marriage works and for what happens when it doesn't work.[8] However, an especially informative source for pastors is Paul Tillich's discussion of the nature of being in vol. 1 of his *Systematic Theology*.[9] Tillich's presentation is certainly theological and philosophical in nature, but I have seen repeatedly in counseling sessions with couples that Tillich's insights are particularly illuminating about the very nature of marriage itself. Pastors will not have to meet many troubled couples before they find themselves encountering exactly what Tillich means about the three polarized pairs of elements that make up the ontological structure of all things, even marriage relationships.

The polarized pairs of elements that will be very apparent in some form in most all marriage counseling situations are *individualization* and *participation*, *dynamics* and *form*, and *freedom* and *destiny*. As polarized pairs, each half of a pair is necessary and essential to the other. Each pole in a pair requires the other pole, which means there is always an inescapable tension between the poles. That is to say that there is no individualization without participation and vice versa, there are no dynamics without form and vice versa, and there is no freedom without destiny and vice versa. It is that same intrinsic tension between the opposite poles that often can be the source of much disturbing tension in marriages, particularly when that tension is not understood and leads to hurt feelings and deepening conflict.

Individualization and Participation

Mark and Evelyn had been married for over twenty-five years and would have said that they had a fulfilling and enriching marriage. They had rented a cabin for a week at a resort on a piece of land that extended like a small peninsula out into a lake. Their cabin was on the west side of the peninsula, and the north end of the peninsula pointed to the lake. On the east side of the small peninsula was the boat dock for the canoes.

Their vacation was to end on Saturday morning. On Friday afternoon they took their rented canoe out for the last time for a ride on the calm lake. As the sun was setting, they were paddling back to their cabin, approaching the peninsula from the east side. As was their custom, Mark paddled from the stern of the canoe so he could steer, and Evelyn paddled from the bow.

As Mark and Evelyn's canoe drew nearer to the peninsula, Mark was surprised by how increasingly difficult it became for him to turn the canoe in the direction of the north end of the peninsula so they could get the canoe around to their cabin. He drove his paddle deeper and deeper into the water on the left side of the canoe, and pushed back on his paddle harder and harder. The canoe would momentarily point toward the end of the peninsula on his right, but then it would immediately lurch back to the left. Mark was confused by the apparent undertow in the lake at this time in the later afternoon. He had never before experienced such a powerful current in this part of the lake! Troubled because he could not direct the canoe to the end of the peninsula, Mark finally brought the problem to Evelyn's attention as she paddled in the bow.

So taken up with his own exertion and anxiety, Mark had not noticed Evelyn driving her own paddle deeper and deeper into the water on the right side of the canoe, and pushing back on her paddle with all her strength. When Mark told Evelyn that a strong undercurrent was moving the canoe away from the north end of the peninsula, Evelyn was dismayed. She had been trying to get the canoe to move to the left toward the boat dock. She told Mark that it made no sense for them to take the canoe back to the cabin since they were leaving in the morning. They might as well leave the canoe at the dock tonight, and there would be one less thing to do in the morning. That was obvious to Evelyn, but it had never occurred to Mark. He was tired and hungry, and he just wanted to get back to the cabin as soon as possible.

Some variation of Mark and Evelyn's experience often occurs in every marriage—two individuals attempting to work together in the same canoe. Elsewhere Tillich offers the observation that "Nietzsche was right when he emphasized that a love relation is creative only if an independent self enters the relation from both sides."[10]

It is the nature of marital love to include a dimension at which both persons have the illusion they and their partner are as inseparable as an infant and mother. Indeed, the infant's perception is that he or she and mother are one with no boundary. Likewise, two very emotionally mature adults married to each other can be quite surprised when they suddenly realize they were expecting and assuming their partner would agree with them and do exactly what they wanted done! There is no getting away from it. Marriage is a union that brings two persons into a mysterious unity where there is often agreement and even ecstasy, but that beautiful experience of unity cannot ever escape the distinctive individuality and uniqueness of each of the partners. Taking account of and affirming the individuality of one's marriage partner is one of the major ongoing tasks of husbands and wives, no matter how long they have been married.

Dynamics and Form

During the evening meal, it became apparent to Tom that Judy was quiet and not her usual talkative self. She seemed to have something on her mind, Tom thought, because she appeared distracted or preoccupied. Finally, Tom asked Judy, "Honey, is something bothering you?"

Tom and Judy had become acquainted in college when Tom was a senior and Judy was a freshman. They met in October, quickly fell in love, and decided the next April that they would get married after Tom graduated in June. Tom was going on to graduate school in another state, which meant that Judy could not finish her college education and would need to get as good a job as she could to help bring in some money to supplement Tom's graduate fellowship. Judy found a job as a hostess in an upscale restaurant for eight dollars an hour. At least it was enough money so they could make it through graduate school.

Now it was eleven years later, and both of their children were in school. Judy had a lot of experience as a mother, but the best job she could get was still in the eight-to-ten-dollar-an-hour range and, frankly, she was bored with clerical jobs. So when Tom asked her if something was bothering her, Judy had to tell him what had been on her mind for more than two months: "Yes, there is something that's been troubling me for several weeks now. Tom, I want to go back to college and finish my B.A. like you did. Then I think I might like to go to law school! I hate to say this, because it will demand a lot of changes for all of us for me to go back to school. Most of all, I want us to be able to work together on new opportunities the future can hold for both of us."

Judy was trying to tell Tom that she was feeling the need for new growth in her life that neither one of them could have anticipated when they married. Tillich's words about the dynamics of change and personal becoming sound as if they were written especially to describe the tensions that are felt in many marriages.

> Therefore, it is impossible to speak of being without also speaking of becoming. Becoming is just as genuine in the structure of being as is

that which remains unchanged in the process of becoming. And, vice versa, becoming would be impossible if nothing were preserved in it as the measure of change.[11]

The original form of Tom and Judy's marriage had been a contract, whether spoken or not but certainly agreed to by both parties at the outset, that Judy would not finish school and would help Tom to get a graduate degree. It was a happy arrangement for both of them. That's why Tom was startled and dismayed to learn that Judy wanted to make some significant changes in their marital and family arrangement. He and Judy had never used the word "contract" with each other, but the sense of betrayal he was feeling was the same betrayal anyone might feel when a trusted partner breaks a solemn agreement.[12]

When most couples get married, they are quite certain that they know their new spouse, that their long conversations have covered all their plans for the future, and that they both know very well what "they are getting into." Indeed, the form of the marriage is set when the pastor declares that they are now husband and wife, and at the very same moment a dynamic process of growth is set in motion as both persons and their relationship continue changing.

The ways both spouses may change, with possible major impacts on their relationship, are virtually limitless. Changes in educational and vocational aspirations are quite common. Changes in personality may also occur as, for example, one spouse takes on a more assertive role in the relationship. Even changes in interests may make a significant difference in a marriage. A wife may declare, "I've spent the last twenty-five years just driving back and forth between home and the office. Now I want to travel and see the rest of the world." Her husband may respond, "I never knew you wanted to travel." She may reply, "I didn't before, but I do now!" Then the question for the marriage becomes whether the husband is also interested in traveling or whether the wife will do her traveling by herself or with friends. That's just the type of question that can bring much tension to a marriage, and it's just the issue that could bring a couple to a pastor's office.

Freedom and Destiny

Sonja reached for another tissue in her pastor's office as she related the awful decision she was facing. Fred had come in late again the night before, about 1:30 a.m. Sonja was, of course, still awake as she heard Fred go to the bathroom and then into the family room, where he fell asleep on the couch. When Sonja confronted him later in the morning, Fred had no explanation for the lipstick on his collar. Sonja gathered up their two preschool children and drove to her girlfriend's house before calling her pastor, who invited Sonja to meet her at the church office.

After listening carefully to Sonja's heartbreaking story, the pastor gently asked, "Sonja, what do you think you should do now for the sake of your marriage, for the sake of your children, and for your own sake?" Sonja sat silently for a couple of long, thoughtful minutes. Then with quiet resolve she looked at her pastor and replied, "I know everyone is telling me to leave Fred, that I'm stupid and just being made a fool of. I've talked to a lawyer, and I know what's involved in getting a legal separation and a divorce. But I'm not leaving. This is the hardest thing I've ever gone through, but I'm not leaving. I'm still going to look at the other options for this mess, other options for the kids, for me, and for this marriage." Then, with her pastor's help, Sonja began the difficult work of deciding what her next steps would be.

Sonja's story is only a variation on the kind of individual decisions many married persons have considered, perhaps many times. An important decision for the marriage doesn't have to be about spousal infidelity. An important decision can be about any issue, however slight or enormous it might appear to others, and it can raise the question of whether or not one wants to continue to be married to one's spouse. Indeed, many retired couples would smile quite knowingly at the line, "I married you for better or for worse, but not for lunch everyday!" People do not have to be married very long to know all too well that even seemingly very small matters can easily trigger the question, "Do I want to be in this marriage?"

That question arises because, according to Tillich's analysis, the very structure of marriage involves an inherent tension between one's freedom and the situation in which one finds oneself. Destiny, says Tillich, "includes the communities to which I belong, the past unremembered and remembered, the environment which has shaped me, the world which has made an impact on me. It refers to all my former decisions."[13] The "community" of one's marriage and the original decision to get married and the ongoing decisions to remain married all make up the destiny or the context within which one finds oneself at the moment. It is exactly within that marital destiny that each spouse also exercises individual freedom in choosing whether to remain within the marriage and, if so, how to participate in the relationship.

Tillich explains that freedom is experienced as deliberation, decision, and responsibility.[14] Deliberation considers the possibilities for action, and decision then settles on a course of action. Even the choice to take no action is a decision. Responsibility means to be accountable for one's decisions, to answer for those decisions. No one else can answer for the decisions we have made in our own freedom. Pastors will often be a witness to husbands and wives struggling deeply with deliberation, decision, and responsibility.

The choice to get married and the wedding ceremony itself all contribute significantly to the destiny of the marriage and the individual destiny of each spouse. These destinies are always in tension with the freedom characteristic of the marriage and each spouse's freedom for deliberation, decision, and responsibility. However, as inescapable as that freedom is, it is just that freedom which offers essential strength and hope for a marriage. Such freedom is the foundational basis for commitment upon which marriages endure for years and decades. The decision to stay in a marriage may be made countless times, but the free basis and character of that decision are what undergird every stable and committed marriage. This is illustrated by a couple, married over forty years, who often throughout those years would reaffirm the depth of their love and individual freedom by saying to each other, "I choose you again!"

Some pastors may be anxious or dismayed by the freedom of choice each spouse has in the marriage. Some pastors may erroneously think they can talk a counselee out of exercising any freedom of choice. Paradoxically, however, pastors can actually uphold the sacredness of the marriage vows while at the same time affirming the fact that a spouse may at any time be deliberating and deciding what to do about those vows. Wise pastors will have come to the realization that it is precisely in affirming the freedom of choice that counselees will be most likely to make their best decisions about the marriage, about any children involved, and about themselves.

The counseling pastor will often recognize the interplay of these three pairs of polarized elements or qualities in the marriages of counselees and parishioners, and even within the pastor's own marriage if the pastor is married. They are essential characteristics that make up the basic nature of every marriage, and the inevitable tensions between the polarities present continuing challenges that couples must deal with in some form at every stage of their marriage. Couples who experience a high level of continuing satisfaction are much more successful in coping with these inherent tensions and challenges. Unhappy and failing marriages often reveal the couples that have found the tensions in these three polarities overwhelming and unmanageable.

The Ten Vital Signs for a Fulfilling Marriage

Sometimes one hears a doctor or nurse refer to a patient's "vital signs," that is, the patient's breathing and pulse rate, temperature, and often blood pressure. In the course of doing professional marriage counseling for twenty-nine years, I identified ten distinctive indicators, or vital signs, for recognizing both healthy marriages and seriously troubled marriages. If there is difficulty with one or two vital signs, there often are significant problems in other areas of the marriage as well. However, troubling stress in just one or two vital sign areas is not necessarily fatal for the future of the marriage, but an indication that the marriage could be in serious trouble. Even a breakdown in several or a majority of the vital sign areas does not have to mean a marriage has no future. Each marriage and the persons in each marriage are unique, as are their capacities for dealing with potentially very divisive marital issues. Therefore, being well aware of the following ten vital signs can aid a pastor in assessing marital strengths and resources as well as identifying more clearly where couples need to focus attention for renewing their relationship.[15] (The ten vital signs are summarized on page 28.)

1. *Love.* It should go without saying that a sound and fulfilling marriage is a loving relationship. Certainly a vital sign for a marriage is whether both partners feel that they are loved, that they are prized and regarded as precious by their spouse.

Most married persons are acutely aware of their own needs in their marriage and the extent to which their spouse meets or fails to meet their various needs. One of the fundamental needs each spouse has is to be loved. But few spouses are aware, either consciously or unconsciously, that their partners married them in order to be loved by them! It is safe to say that most people decide to marry another person because they feel particularly loved in the presence of that person. They feel deeply, warmly, and affectionately accepted by the other person more than by anyone else. The other person knows them and many of their secrets more than anyone else does and, amazingly, does not reject them. So we marry that person, because for the rest of our life we want to be loved by that person. But few married persons ever give it much, if any, thought that that is why their partner married them: to be loved by them!

Love is shown in many ways, often by little signs and expressions of appreciation and affection. The lack of love in a marriage relationship is painfully felt by both spouses and often is quite evident to friends and other family members. Continuing indifference, hostility, arguing, and sarcastic references, as well as the withholding of physical attention and affection, are some of the indicators of a marriage that has ceased to be a loving union. This is a serious vital sign, but not necessarily a fatal sign for the marriage if the couple is motivated to do the necessary work toward reconciliation.

2. *Trust.* Nothing is more essential to a satisfying and fulfilling marriage, and more fragile and harder to restore, than basic trust between partners. In hardly any other continuing human relationship are two people more vulnerable to each other—physically, emotionally, and, in many cases, financially. In hardly any other human relationship can partners in the relationship potentially suffer more pain than in a marriage. Indeed, there is very likely no greater symbol of marital vulnerability than to sleep in the same bed. Certainly you don't close your eyes and fall asleep if you don't trust your bed partner!

Marital trust can be threatened or shattered by physical or sexual abuse, infidelity or flirtatious behavior, alcohol or other drug abuse, emotional instability, and by financial irresponsibility or gambling. Moreover, once marital trust is lost or threatened, it can be difficult to recover. For example, even a single incident of physical abuse early in a marriage can have lingering damaging effects for decades. The abuser most often does not understand how difficult it is to recover trust, and will frequently try to dismiss or diminish the significance of the abusive event. "I hit you over fifteen years ago—what's your problem now? Why don't you get over it?" Or a spouse who had been involved in an extramarital affair may bristle at having to continue to "prove" trustworthiness by reporting his or her whereabouts and being prompt in returning home when expected.

The course of recovery and rebuilding of broken trust cannot be predicted from one marriage to another. For some "offended" spouses, trust may be restored over a relatively brief time or the period of recovery may require years. Such recovery is not a matter of will power by the "offended" spouse to decide, "As of this moment, I will now trust Carolyn." Rather, trust has both a cognitive, decision-making element and an emotional component, which are both deeply affected by the dynamics of the marital relationship. This is to say that marital trust is too complex to be amenable to a quick fix. But the marriage that reflects a sound, basic trust between both partners has a very promising foundation from which to meet other marital challenges.

3. *Commitment.* Often a pastoral counselor will do well to ask each spouse in the first counseling session, after all the problems and complaints have been outlined, "Do you still want to be married to your

spouse?" The question goes directly to a very important vital sign. No matter what the current crises and tensions may be in a marriage, there is much hope for the future of the relationship if they can say to the other, "I still want to be married to you."

Of course, a negative response from either spouse may reflect an impulsive frustration over a current crisis and not really disclose deeper, more reasoned feelings. On the other hand, it is not unusual for a spouse who has endured months and years of marital unhappiness to have already reached the decision no longer to continue in the marriage. So when the reply is, "No, I am sorry, but I do not want to be married to you," the other spouse may be hearing for the first time shocking but very important information.

Asking in the first session whether they still want to be married is important mainly so that each spouse knows the other's intention about the marriage. If there has been denial by one of the spouses about the seriousness of the marital problems, a negative reply from the other may finally help that spouse to recognize painful realities that have been avoided or dismissed. Another important reason for asking the question in the first session is that, consciously or unconsciously, some spouses who have already decided to end the marriage use the marriage counseling process to let the other person down gently. In other words, they engage in marriage counseling as a pretense for somehow eventually conveying the bad news that the marriage is over. At the same time, the other spouse has the reinforced false hope that, because they are both going to marriage counseling, both of them want to reconcile and make the marriage work. Such pretense in fact uses the pastor and the counseling to build up the other spouse's false hopes.

When both spouses can still affirm to each other that they want to remain married, regardless of all the marital pain they may be feeling at the moment, there are hardly any marital problems that cannot somehow be resolved and reconciled. That is why this is such an important vital sign. Likewise, if either spouse has decided that the marriage is over, there is little likelihood that any progress can be made. A pastor will be wise in such circumstances to encourage neither spouse to make any immediate final decisions, and to allow some time for further discussions with each other and with the pastor before taking steps toward dissolution of the marriage.

4. *Companionship.* Spouses who have a satisfying and fulfilling marriage will report that they enjoy doing things together with their partner. That is not to say that married couples should do everything together. Indeed,

a significant aspect of affirming one's own individuality in a marriage is to have activities and friendships with others that do not include one's spouse. But a satisfying marriage will be characterized by two persons who enjoy spending time with each other, working on projects together, and talking with each other. Indeed, it is the strongly felt need for companionship that motivates most widows and widowers to consider remarriage. Howard and Charlotte Clinebell quote a husband whose words describe the vital essence of companionship in a fulfilling marriage: "The things we do together aren't fun intrinsically—the ecstasy comes from *being together in the doing.* Take her out of the picture and I wouldn't give a damn for the boat, the lake, or any of the fun that goes on there."[16]

Much marital companionship is hardly ever about ecstasy. A billboard along Interstate 10 in Southern California once showed a retired couple standing with their arms around each other on a golf course with the caption, "An enchanted moment!" Despite the advertising, companionship is not always about enchanted moments. Rather, companionship is the deep sense of satisfaction and fulfillment of being with the person you most want to be with more than anyone else. And companionship is always accompanied with an abiding sense of wonder that this person, who knows you and all your faults better than anyone else, still wants to be with you in so many of the adventures that make up life's journey together. Companionship expresses one of the deepest levels of acceptance in marriage.

Troubled couples don't experience much companionship. Even if they are engaged in an activity together, they still aren't together, because they don't enjoy each other's company and may even feel ill at ease being with each other. It certainly can help if two spouses have a number of common areas of interest. But two people who *want* to be with each other will always find common areas of mutual enjoyment. On the other hand, having many common interests does not necessarily guarantee that a couple will enjoy much companionship. Pastoral counselors should inquire what a couple enjoys doing together so they can be with each other and in each other's presence. Where meaningful and satisfying marital companionship is not experienced and reported by both spouses, very likely the relationship needs serious attention and work if it is to survive.

5. *Justice and fairness.* In a satisfying and fulfilling marriage, both spouses feel that there is an equal or very nearly equal sharing of effort, responsibility, and commitment in the relationship. It does not matter how the marital relationship may appear to outside observers, who may think one or the other of the spouses does very little compared to all the

work done by the other spouse for the marriage and home. The assessment that matters is that of each of the marriage partners.

Likewise, the lack of perceived fairness in the marriage is a common indicator of marital breakdown. This theme may be heard in a variety of complaints: "You spend hours surfing the Internet while I have to put the kids to bed," "I work hard all day to bring home a decent salary, and you can't even keep the house clean," "I cook the meals, but you never clean up the table afterward," and "I pay my half of the bills out of my checking account, but you don't keep up with the bills you promised to pay out of your checking account."

If both spouses do not feel that the marriage relationship is essentially fair and just, invariably at some level there will be attempts "to get even," to correct the injustice. Most often the getting even will be harmful or destructive to the marriage. Sarcasm, angry flare-ups, the withholding of affection and sex, withdrawing into silence, shopping sprees, and flirting outside the marriage or having an affair are examples that can be conscious or unconscious attempts to correct a deeply felt injustice.

Pastoral counselors will often find themselves helping troubled couples address concerns over relationship injustice. Such perceptions of unfairness need to be taken very seriously by the counselor and never dismissed, no matter how insignificant they may appear to an outsider. Fortunately, in most marriages where there is a desire to remain married, perceptions and feelings of relationship injustice can be addressed and resolved to the satisfaction of both spouses. Such resolution may take much hard work, but most couples can achieve satisfaction in the area of this vital sign where there is basic commitment to their marriage.

6. *The respectful negotiation of power.* Power in a relationship is the capacity each person has to exert influence upon the other member of the relationship. In a marriage, both spouses are continually exerting and negotiating their power to influence each other. A grown woman once reported an incident that occurred in her family when she was a young girl. She was very interested when a salesman came to their home in the afternoon to demonstrate a new vacuum cleaner to her mother. It was obvious to the young girl that the vacuum cleaner impressed her mother, and she exclaimed, "Let's tell Daddy when he comes home!" But her mother made it clear that telling Daddy should be left to Mother's sense of the proper time. That evening it was difficult for the girl to say nothing all through dinner about the vacuum cleaner. Moreover, she couldn't understand why her mother didn't say anything about something so important. But the girl did observe that they had her father's favorite meal:

roast beef with mashed potatoes and gravy. Also, she was surprised that her mother had also prepared a special dessert—again, her father's favorite—of sliced peaches with ice cream. It was only after her father had finished his dessert that her mother finally brought up the subject of the vacuum cleaner, which her father agreed would be a wise purchase. The woman who reported this event also said that in her family the father was the "head of the house" but her mother was the "neck that turned the head"!

Pastoral counselors will readily recognize how both spouses have the power to influence the behavior of their partner in almost limitless ways. The negotiation of that power may be openly discussed by some couples, though most often the power that is exercised in a marriage is rarely examined or talked about.

The destructive expression of power in a marriage often occurs through sexual or physical abuse as well as through emotional assault and manipulation, whether overtly or silently. Intimidating abuse may be expressed by shouting and verbal outbursts, the breaking or throwing of objects, and the repeated slamming of doors. Likewise, the display of a weapon or a threat upon the other's life is a violent abuse of power in a marriage.

In a satisfying and fulfilling marriage, a fundamental respect is felt by each spouse from the other spouse, without manipulative, intimidating, or abusive power. Such respect is an essential vital sign that shows much promise for the future of a marriage. Where basic and affectionate respect is lacking in a marriage, this vital sign reflects significant trouble for a marriage. A sensitive pastor will listen carefully for evidence that both spouses recognize their capacity to exert power and that they use such powerful influence to be respectful and caring while working through their issues and problems.

7. *Effective and caring communication.* How a wife and husband talk to each other is one of the most important vital signs of a marriage. In nearly all of the couples seen by professional marriage counselors, the communication between spouses has become destructive, making it nearly impossible for spouses to discuss their relationship issues, much less work through those issues to reconciliation. In most seriously conflicted marriages, "molehills" quickly escalate into "mountains" as defensive and attacking styles of communication fuel the eruption of antagonism and bitterness. By the same token, the originally troubling issues for most couples can be worked through in a constructive and productive manner when effective and caring approaches to communication are used.

A marital relationship is one of the most, if not the most, emotionally intensive relationships humans ever experience. Strong feelings, often to the surprise of the spouses, can break out almost with no warning at all and erupt even over seemingly trivial matters. When humans have strong feelings, we naturally and typically resort to language and patterns of speaking that only compound the problem instead of easing tensions. For example, when we are angry, frustrated, or hurt, or when we feel we are being accused or attacked, we instinctively use "you" language to blame, question, or somehow characterize the other person. The pastoral counselor will often hear such defensive and blaming language when listening to troubled and conflicted couples.

Indeed, much of the focus of professional marriage counseling is to defuse the argumentative verbal exchanges between the pair and to help them hear each other's concerns and issues without responding with impulsive defensive challenges and accusations. Effective communication that facilitates listening and nonaccusatory responses is a very important vital sign indicating a satisfying marriage. That is not to say that such marriages never have troubling issues. They do. But when a couple is faced with such issues, the ability for both spouses to listen carefully and to respond without attacking, blaming, or questioning will make it all the more likely for that couple constructively to resolve most any issue.

8. *Self-responsibility and self-differentiation.* Another important vital sign is the capacity for both spouses to affirm and permit separateness, individuality, and responsibility for one's self in the marriage. This vital sign will take on different expressions in different marriages. But when there is excessive emotional dependence, the marriage relationship can experience much strain.

A notable example of excessive emotional dependence is the popular romantic myth that a husband and wife are to "make each other happy." A husband looked at his counselor and lamented that it seemed to him that he and his wife weren't doing a very good job of making each other happy. The counselor asked if they had made that promise to each other in their marriage vows. The counselor did not know of any marriage vows that include the clause, "And I promise to make you happy as long as we both shall live." To the counselor's surprise and dismay, the young man replied in all seriousness, "Oh yes, in our vows we promised to make each other happy!"

An exact and useful definition of "happy" is elusive, even with a dictionary definition such as "enjoying or characterized by well-being and contentment."[17] Such a definition suggests an image of one spouse lying back in a lounge chair on Super Bowl Sunday while the other, like a dutiful servant, brings popcorn, chips, and whatever drinks are requested. This scenario is hard to imagine if the goal is for two spouses to keep each other contented like that all the time. Indeed, while devoted love requires being thoughtful and caring, it is not possible for one person to make another person happy, and most especially if the other person doesn't want to be happy.

Happiness is the result of an inner decision and conviction regarding oneself and one's expectations about one's environment and situation. Happiness is up to one's own making, and expecting one's spouse to be responsible for one's own happiness is a setup for profound disappointment and frustration in the marriage. Indeed, it is entirely possible that a spouse who takes on a servant role dedicated to keeping the other happy may as a result cease to remain attractive to the other spouse. In fact, strange as it may seem, it can even become annoying having someone around all the time who is constantly trying to make us happy.

Another symptom of stress in this vital sign is when one spouse assumes responsibility for the psychological self-esteem and well-being of the other spouse. The first spouse takes on the role of "resident psychologist," offering precise analyses, ordinarily unrequested, about the flaws in the other's personality and what the other spouse should do to develop greater self-esteem or otherwise improve his or her general mental health. A marriage has a greater chance for deepening satisfaction when spouses are their own "psychologist" and take responsibility for their own mental health. The obvious exception to this guideline is when a spouse is a serious threat to self or others and requires emergency intervention and possible hospitalization.

Spouses will partner and work together on many tasks in their marriage, from rearing the children to grocery shopping to making decisions about the next vacation or when to entertain. Furthermore, it is not uncommon for each spouse to assume certain roles on a continuing basis, so that, for example, one spouse usually looks after the care and maintenance of the family car while another spouse takes the lead in paying the bills. Mutual support and teamwork are necessary to a viable and satisfying marriage. But excessive dependence can become very burdensome in a marriage. For example, Gerald worked out of the home from an office he had set up in his basement. While this arrangement had some obvious benefits for convenience and setting his own work hours, working out of the home came to reinforce Gerald's increasing dependence on his wife, Doris. Before, when Gerald went to an office, Doris would choose Gerald's clothes and lay them out on the bed each morning. She fixed Gerald's breakfast. He bought his lunch at the office cafeteria, but came home to an evening meal prepared by Doris. Now that he was working out of his basement, Doris still laid out his clothes in the morning and now prepared all three of Gerald's meals. Indeed, Gerald was petrified by any thought of preparing any meal for himself in the kitchen. If Doris had any engagements in the morning or the afternoon away from the home, she had to make sure that she was either at home at noon to prepare Gerald's lunch, or she had to have it prepared in advance so he could eat it without any effort on his part. Doris was clearly exasperated by her resulting loss of independence. When the counselor gently suggested to Gerald that he begin preparing just one meal for himself during the week, even shopping ahead of time for the necessary ingredients for the meal, Gerald's eyes filled with panic. Gerald feared the truth that both he and Doris knew all too well: He could no longer take care of himself. Greater satisfaction is to be found in marriages where each spouse has not lost the capacity to care for herself or himself, and where each spouse is responsible, finally, for her or his own joy and satisfaction with her or his own self and life.

9. *Sexual fulfillment.* In spite of all the research and all the books written on human sexuality in the last fifty years, the sexual and pleasure bonding between spouses is a vital dimension of marriage that still defies adequate comprehension or explanation. Likewise, spouses still have difficulty understanding their own sexuality, much less their partner's sexual needs and functioning. As soon as we think we understand ourself and our partner, if we are honest, we soon discover we aren't as smart as we thought we were.

Satisfying sexual intimacy is a very complex marital interaction. Wives and husbands soon learn that their bodies and their sexual needs and appetites—indeed, the meaning of sexual relating—differ very much from the other's. In fact, attempting to relate sexually with each other is complicated furthermore because one cannot avoid the perspective of one's own sexuality. He will try to understand her sexuality from his viewpoint as a man, and she can only attempt to understand his sexuality from her viewpoint as a woman. The almost unlimited potential for misunderstanding on both sides is all too obvious!

Despite the inherent complexities, essential satisfaction with one's sexual relationship with one's spouse is a necessary vital sign for a marriage. Such satisfaction cannot be measured by the standards proposed by some recent poll or what hundreds of other couples report they are doing or how often they do it. Essential sexual satisfaction in a marriage can only be measured by the needs of each spouse and the extent to which those needs are met. Those needs can be affected by a host of dynamics in a relationship, by demands being made upon a marriage by external factors such as children and job pressures, and by the couple's stage of life. For example, as couples grow older they are likely to note changes in the frequency and expression of their sexual relationship. Furthermore, obstacles to sexual satisfaction may be solely attributable to relationship dynamics, and other impediments to satisfactory sexual functioning may be due completely to bodily dysfunctions. Unfortunately, many married couples find their sexual relationship to be the most difficult aspect of their marriage to discuss openly with care and mutual understanding.

Satisfactory sexual relating in a marriage is an essential vital sign, though good sex alone is not enough to sustain an enduring relationship. When sexual tension is distracting a couple from fully enjoying their marriage, but where there is loving commitment to each other—and often the help of a professional therapist—new understandings and behaviors can lead to a level of sexual pleasure and satisfaction that will reinforce a deepening marital relationship.

10. *Shared spiritual values.* The day is past in most faith traditions when clergy refuse to participate in a wedding ceremony involving a spouse from another tradition. It is not extraordinary now for Catholic and Protestant clergy to take part in the same marriage ceremony, nor is it unusual for Jews and Christians to marry, or even Muslims and Christians.

More important than membership in organized religious institutions is the sharing of similar spiritual values regarding ultimate meanings, ultimate commitments, and ultimate principles for living one's life, as well as some agreement about religious practices. Couples who have common spiritual values and practices have a unique foundation for their relationship that will be an invaluable resource when facing the inevitable stresses that come to every marriage. On the other hand, the lack of shared religious commitments does not necessarily doom a marriage to failure. In fact, there are many apparently satisfying marriages where church is not attended and spiritual matters are never discussed. But where shared spiritual values are missing, a couple is without a vital sign that could otherwise offer great potential for enriching and undergirding a marriage for many years of fulfillment and satisfaction. The sensitive and caring pastoral counselor will talk about the shared spiritual values held by couples, being careful not to impose religious constraints while inviting couples to explore and discuss their own shared ultimate values and commitments.

Pastoral Marriage Counseling:
A Hopeful Dialogue

The Hopeful Pastoral Counseling Process

The question might fairly be asked by pastors, "What's the use in trying to get unhappy couples to sit down together in my office?" While a number of responses might be given to that question, this counselor has repeatedly observed the hopeful and constructive potential and promise when even the most conflicted persons have the opportunity to engage in a respectful dialogue in a structured setting. The intrinsic character of dialogue makes it possible for intimate, committed relationships to be transformed in positive and hopeful ways and often in directions neither person had anticipated.[18]

Two particular writers have offered insights about the rich potential of dialogue that can be very informative for the counseling pastor who sees conflicted couples. Martin Buber, a Jewish philosopher, is perhaps best known for his exposition of the "dialogical principle" in his classic work *I and Thou*. Buber's analysis of the encounter between two persons in dialogue led him to three important conclusions for pastoral counselors working with couples to consider. First, the *I-Thou* encounter of dialogue envisioned by Buber requires the participation of one's total being, which inherently must involve risk: "This is the risk: the primary word (*I-Thou*) can only be spoken with the whole being."[19]

Second, Buber clarifies how dialogue requires a kind of listening to the other person that does not jeopardize the listener's own experience. Buber preferred to call such listening "inclusion" instead of "empathy," because inclusion can "live through" the common event from the other's standpoint without relinquishing one's own reality.[20] Third, Buber was compelled to recognize that where such dialogue occurs, where two or more persons truly and honestly and openly encounter each other, God is present. Buber says it this way: "Only when two say to one another with all that they are, 'It is *Thou*,' is the indwelling of the Present Being between them."[21]

Though Buber wrote as a Jew, Christians will have little difficulty recognizing the eternal Dialogue with us humans through the incarnation, God risking God's self through Jesus Christ's fully taking upon himself our human form. God has defined the essence of dialogue through the Christ event, in which God is fully present in order lovingly to call all human beings to be fully themselves. That is why the incarnation is the preeminent, reconciling miracle of dialogue. Christians can believe that wherever dialogue takes place—particularly earnest, risking, and open dialogue that engages the whole being of husband and wife—God is present to call them to be reconciled to each other, to be more fully present to each other, and to be more fully themselves through their relationship. Of course, when that occurs, Christians should have no trouble at all recognizing it as a miracle. Likewise, it is the potential for just that kind of miracle that makes pastoral marriage counseling such a hopeful and exciting enterprise!

The other writer, Reuel Howe, is an important interpreter of Martin Buber. At the outset of his book *The Miracle of Dialogue*, Howe includes marriage as one of his examples for the importance of dialogue. He declares that dialogical marriage is particularly nonexploitive:

> Healing of a marriage or any other relationship cannot occur when the partners see themselves as separate individuals with a right to demand services of each other. Healing can come only when one or the other is able to turn toward his [*sic*] partner, to accept the risk of giving himself in love, and to search himself for whatever reform may be necessary. A wife, for example, may be able to make this kind of gift, and yet have it fail to heal because her husband cannot accept her gift and give himself in return. But if he can, then the miracle will occur and the dead relationship will be called again into life.[22]

This is the exciting hope for every failing or dead relationship, an empowering hope grounded in reality, that is promised when a pastor creates a respectful, structured context for marital dialogue through the short-term marriage counseling plan. Andrew Lester summarizes well the essence of such hope for conflicted couples:

> Hope does *not* function as an opiate that causes people to deny reality. In fact, hope provides the courage to face whatever chaos and trauma life throws at us. . . . Hope assumes the future contains potentialities not visible in the present.[23]

The Hopeful Dialogical Pastor

The encouraging marital dialogue takes place in the presence of a pastor who functions as a hopeful dialogical person. Reuel Howe offers a challenge to all Christians that isn't confined to pastors, but his observation is especially relevant to the pastoral marriage counselor: "It is imperative, then, that a Christian be a dialogical person through whom the Word that gives life is spoken."[24] Howe notes four particular characteristics of the dialogical person, characteristics that will especially enable the pastor to facilitate the dialogical conversation between husband and wife.[25]

1. The dialogical person is a total, authentic person who is really present as a listener and does not "run off on errands" in his or her mind while appearing to listen.
2. The dialogical person is an open person who will appropriately reveal herself or himself while also being open to receiving what is disclosed by others. In other words, the pastor does not permit her or his own defensiveness to be an obstacle to honest and revealing communication, and thus can be more open to the depth of meaning present in the counseling setting.
3. The dialogical person is a disciplined person who has learned through professional and personal maturity when to speak and when not to speak. Howe calls it a matter of accepting "the limitations as well as the opportunities the relationship offers."[26]
4. The dialogical person is a related person who believes the greatest gain is to be found through relatedness with others. Instead of manipulating relationships to protect himself or herself from involvement, the dialogical pastor believes that the benefits of relationship always outweigh the risks of misunderstanding and alienation.

Therefore, there is no surprise that dialogue always offers the potential for new beginnings, even beginnings that could never have been anticipated: "It is in dialogue that acceptance is given and received. The word spoken in dialogue is an act of faith done in spite of the doubt that it will do any good. The dialogical word is an open word, a word of beginnings, because it is a word of expectation inviting response."[27]

The source of all hope for the pastor and for troubled couples is that God, in a way defying explanation, is fully present in every dialogue. Sometimes God's presence may be very difficult for a pastor and a couple to discern. All the pain and hurt that frequently is expressed between spouses may make it very difficult to believe that God is present in a conversation marked by conflict. But God is surely present, just as present as on occasions when a pastor may be aware that she or he is "on holy ground" in the presence of honest and caring marital dialogue, holy ground that always holds the promise for reconciliation and healing!

*Pastoral Attitudes and Behaviors That Facilitate
a Hopeful Marital Dialogue*

Counseling pastors can do much about their own attitudes and their own behaviors that will encourage the kind of marital dialogue envisioned by Buber and Howe. Wayne Oates, for example, has identified three essential characteristics of a helping relationship: accurate empathy, nonpossessive warmth, and an inherent genuineness.[28] Accurate empathy is able to convey a very close understanding of another's issues. Nonpossessive warmth is an authentic expression of caring without any conditions or strings attached, and genuineness communicates honesty and integrity toward others and about one's own self and feelings. These pastoral qualities and behaviors will greatly enhance the potential for a couple to have a productive and promising counseling dialogue.

The effective pastoral counselor who sensitively encourages healing and a hope-filled, reconciling dialogue will also have many of the following:

> *A genuine liking for people.* Parishioners will know immediately that their pastor affirms them, cares for them, and is concerned about their troubles and burdens.
>
> *An essentially positive feeling of self-worth.* Such a pastor will be less likely to measure personal self-worth by "success" as a marriage counselor.
>
> *An awareness of one's own feelings* and the ability to value them instead of discounting them.
>
> *The ability to set boundaries* in a professional manner, particularly for such things as the length and frequency of counseling sessions and of telephone conversations.
>
> *The ability to live with ambiguity* and unresolved conflict in others' marriages, knowing that despite one's best efforts as a counselor, not all couples will be helped.
>
> *Sufficient self-esteem and courage* to be both honest and appropriately assertive.
>
> *The ability to communicate and tell the truth* in ways that typically invite receptivity instead of defensiveness.
>
> *A personal social support network* so that counseling relationships are not used inappropriately as the pastor's social relationships. Furthermore, if a pastor is married, a growing and fulfilling marriage

at home, coupled with some understanding of the deeper dynamics of his or her own marriage, is an essential asset to ensure that a pastor does not work out his or her own marriage problems through misguided counseling.

The willingness to use outside persons or resources for consultation about counseling cases and situations.

A commitment to be a counselor to both spouses without taking sides.

A sense of prayer upon entering the counseling relationship.

Conclusion

The model for pastoral marriage counseling to be discussed in the following chapters is grounded in the hopeful promise of a structured marital dialogue facilitated by a pastor. The hope is always realistic, but it never lets so-called realism prematurely shut the door on possibilities. The model never loses sight of the limited resources a pastor brings to the enterprise of marriage counseling. The model recognizes the obvious constraints of a short-term counseling model with a specific number of sessions. However, the model also affirms the strengths inherent in short-term counseling, especially by directing a couple's focused attention toward the three possible outcomes for the counseling, outcomes openly and clearly discussed and anticipated from the outset of the counseling. And, despite all the challenges faced by a pastor and a couple, pastoral marriage counseling that encourages the meeting of *I* and *Thou* in respectful and self-disclosing dialogue will always offer the hopeful possibility for new understanding and insight leading to reconciliation and even promising relationship options no one could have envisioned. Our God who is always present in loving dialogue through Jesus Christ is the ground for such hopeful expectations, which surely can empower every pastor to say confidently to troubled couples, "I have a plan!"

Ten Vital Signs for a Satisfying and Growing Marriage

1. *Love.* Central to the marriage relationship is the undoubted assurance both spouses have of feeling deeply, warmly, and affectionately accepted by their marriage partner.
2. *Trust.* Both spouses feel safe and secure with each other's decisions and behavior toward them physically, emotionally, sexually, and financially.
3. *Commitment.* No matter how much pain a marriage has experienced in the past, if both spouses still want to be married, there is much hope for the relationship.
4. *Companionship.* A wife and a husband will have other friends they each enjoy by themselves, but most meaningful and fulfilling are the times when they are in each other's presence. They like to be together, and when they aren't together, they anticipate the next time when they will be with each other.
5. *Justice and fairness.* For a marriage to be fulfilling with potential for continuing growth, both persons need to feel that the relationship is fair and that neither is benefiting more than the other.
6. *The respectful negotiation of power.* In a healthy marriage neither spouse feels intimidated, bullied, or otherwise manipulated by the other.
7. *Effective and caring communication.* Marital dialogue that avoids blaming and arguing while demonstrating genuine listening is essential to dealing with the marital differences that arise for every couple.
8. *Self-responsibility and self-differentiation.* A marriage has greater promise for stability and growth in intimacy when both spouses have a firm sense of their own identity and capabilities apart from all that the other spouse brings to the marriage.
9. *Sexual fulfillment.* Sexual needs and practices evolve and change for couples over the years, and in a fulfilling marriage there is continuing satisfaction about how each other's changing sexual needs are respected and honored.
10. *Shared spiritual values.* The more that a couple can affirm and talk about mutual spiritual needs and interests, the greater the potential will be for deeper intimacy in the marriage.

Chapter Two

Putting the Plan into Action

In our experience any couple may reach a crisis point, often related to internal changes in one or both partners or to external life-related events impinging on the couple that catapult people into outdated, non-problem-solving feelings, thoughts and behaviors. An appropriately placed and directed series of interventions into this unhelpful, often archaic interlocking process is frequently sufficient for couples again to touch into their love for one another and explore other cooperative solutions to problems.

—Maria Gilbert and Diana Shmukler,
Brief Therapy with Couples: An Integrative Approach

This chapter covers:

~ A discussion of the counseling plan
~ Working the plan with a couple
~ Six steps for the first session
~ A checklist for effective counseling
~ When all doesn't go as planned

Pastor Barbara Cowan keeps her word. Two days later in the evening she makes a telephone call to her parishioners, Ron and Mary Nelson. She feels a little nervous, because she does not know how Ron and Mary will respond. On the other hand, she knows that she has a positive plan that can be a constructive pastoral intervention to help her parishioners. She hopes that Ron will answer the telephone. He does, and she begins: "Hello, Ron. This is Barbara Cowan calling from church. I'm calling because Mary and I were talking briefly after the meeting two nights ago, and she was sharing some real concerns about how things are going for the two of you and your marriage. We didn't talk about any details, but I told Mary that I would like for the three of us—you, Mary, and me—to sit down together in my office to talk about the concerns both of you have. I'm calling to see if we could set up a time for us to get together."

Pastor Cowan might have asked the customary introductory question, "How are you doing?" but she engages in little or no small talk and moves directly to the point of her call. She also does not use qualifiers such as "just," "maybe," "might sometime," or "kind of" to diminish or soften the significance of her call—"I'm *just* calling because . . . ," or "*maybe* we could get together in my office," or "*might sometime* have a meeting to *kind of* talk about your marriage." Nor does Pastor Cowan begin with, "I don't know if Mary had a chance to talk with you yet." Pastor Cowan is pastoral and direct to the point, instead of trying somehow to manipulate Ron's response.

Ron's reply might be negative. He could say that he is not interested, or he might say that he and Mary discussed the matter and decided that there is nothing to talk over with Pastor Cowan. The pastor may gently challenge Ron's response by saying, "Mary certainly sounded concerned when she and I were talking after the meeting. That's why I wanted to be sure to call tonight." Pastor Cowan has shown that she takes Mary's concerns seriously. But if Ron indicates no further interest in a meeting with her, then Pastor Cowan will assure Ron that she will be glad to be available at any time in the future if there is any way he and Mary feel she might be helpful. Thus, Pastor Cowan has respected her parishioners' right to say no while also conveying her intention to continue to be their concerned and attentive pastor. Pastor Cowan makes a mental note to watch and listen carefully for any further signs or evidence of marital stress between Ron and Mary when she might once again have the opportunity to invite them both to meet with her.

If, however, the response from Ron is positive, Pastor Cowan makes an appointment to see both Ron and Mary in her office at the church. Ron might say that he wants to talk with her alone first because he feels that she has already heard Mary's side of the story, which he assumes puts him in a bad light. But Pastor Cowan does not honor Ron's request for a prior individual session. She kindly but firmly states that Mary really did not go into any details in the parking lot, and that she wants to hear from both of them together because their marriage obviously involves both of them. Pastor Cowan may add that at a later time she will plan to talk with each of them separately, but not at the moment.

Brief Pastoral Marriage Counseling

By far the counseling that is done most of the time by parish pastors is of a short-term nature, consisting of ten or fewer sessions and often only two or three sessions. Clergy do not have the time to devote to longer counseling commitments, and very few clergy have the clinical training and background to engage in longer-term counseling and to manage the transference and countertransference relationship issues that typically arise with such intensive counseling relationships. But that does not mean that the shorter-term, brief counseling done by most parish pastors is less effective than longer-term counseling models. Howard Stone has made the compelling argument that pastors have no reason to feel that their counseling interventions are less effective than the longer-term counseling done by other mental health professionals. In Stone's book on short-term counseling he asserts:

> The viewpoint presented in this book is that brief pastoral counseling methods, for most people encountered in the parish, are not only as good as longer methods but are actually better because they take less time and are equally effective. This fact alone suggests that brief methods should be the approach of first choice for clergy in congregational settings.[1]

Nonetheless, despite a wide recognition in the pastoral care literature that short-term counseling is preferable in the parish context, Stone concludes his survey of the brief counseling literature with a sharp critique of the failure of writers to offer short-term counseling models to pastors for helping marriages and families.

> Given that many of the proponents of brief counseling have come from marriage and family therapy, it may be that pastoral counseling theorists have tended not to embrace brief counseling because of their ties to individual rather than systems-oriented theory and methods. For parish pastors this means that, though they care for couple and family difficulties more than any other type of problem,

the pastoral counseling books they read are primarily individual in orientation. Once again, the literature of pastoral counseling is out of touch with the context of congregational ministry.[2]

However, a major premise of this book is that a structured, short-term approach to troubled marriages is particularly well suited to the parish setting especially because of important factors pastors bring to the counseling session that other mental health professionals cannot offer. The role of the pastor in the church, in the community, and in parishioners' lives carries with it a palpable authority regardless of how unauthoritative the pastor may try to be. Though pastoral authority is widely questioned and challenged by many, most counselees will regard the pastor as a significant spiritual figure or mentor in their life. Indeed, the pastor's spiritual authority is due to the fact that the pastor represents the heritage of such foundational Judeo-Christian values as love, trust, justice, forgiveness, and reconciliation.[3] In seeing a pastor in the church office, parishioners are at some level confronted and supported by those faith values in a way much less likely experienced when seeing other counselors in a secular setting such as a professional office suite or a mental health center. Most pastors will also have a caring attitude and loving concern undergirded with the wisdom from years of experience and observation of human behavior. And many pastors now will have had some formal counseling or pastoral care training in such settings as Clinical Pastoral Education (CPE). Parish pastors have more than enough to offer to troubled couples when they assuredly say to them, "I have a plan to help you turn your marriage around and make hopeful decisions for yourselves and for your family."

The Plan

Brief pastoral marriage counseling can be done effectively by following a structured five-stage model that involves five to seven sessions with the couple, both individually and together. The sessions typically last from fifty to sixty minutes and are generally scheduled once a week.

1. *The invitation to couple counseling.* Through contact initiated by themselves or their pastor, one or both spouses make it known that their marriage is in trouble or has some significant problems. The pastor invites the couple to come together to the first marriage counseling session in the pastor's office.

2. *The initial session with the couple.* Both spouses are seen together so

they can discuss with their pastor in each other's presence the problems that are causing conflict or tension in their relationship. The pastor offers the plan for marriage counseling and invites the couple to formalize their intention to work together to resolve the problems in their relationship by signing the Covenant for Pastoral Marriage Counseling (CPMC; see appendix A). The couple understands that the pastor will recommend one of three options at the final session. In preparation for the following sessions, the pastor gives each spouse the Pastoral Marriage Counseling Questionnaire (PMCQ; see appendix B), which will elicit essential background information about each partner and about their relationship.

3. *Individual sessions with each spouse.* The pastor sees each spouse separately for one or two counseling sessions.

4. *Both spouses seen together.* In a single session, the pastor helps the couple assess the insights they have gained thus far in the counseling process. The pastor and the couple decide upon a growth task for the couple to work on before the final session, as a step toward the improvement of their relationship.

5. *The final session.* The purpose of this session is for the pastor and the couple to evaluate the progress made toward resolving marital concerns and problems. At this meeting the pastor will recommend one of three options: termination of counseling, referral to another counselor or therapist, or recontracting with the pastor for no more than three additional marriage counseling sessions.

The Invitation to Couple Counseling

In many instances the pastor's invitation will begin the process through which a couple engages in marital counseling. Situations like Pastor Cowan's late evening conversation in the church parking lot will often be the unforeseen occasion when a pastor learns that a couple might well benefit from marriage counseling. James Dittes rightly notes, "Most pastoral counseling comes by surprise and in disguise, not by appointment and clearly separated from non-counseling encounters."[4] Pastors may learn about marital stresses in the course of any conversation at the church or while making a pastoral call for other purposes in a home or in the hospital. Indeed, this is one of the most striking advantages parish pastors have that the other helping professions do not have. Parish clergy have extensive access to a wide range of the population that otherwise might never come to the attention of other professionals, certainly to the attention of mental health counselors and marriage and family therapists.

Creating a Pastoral Context for the Invitation

Some pastors report that there are no marriage problems in their congregation and that, therefore, they never have any need to offer counseling to troubled couples. On the other hand, there are other pastors who say that their counseling load just continues to grow and that they have had to set sharp limits to their counseling hours so they can attend to other responsibilities. There are many factors that can contribute to those opposite scenarios. Pastors and their congregations should examine the messages being sent to parishioners about their marriages and the educational enrichment opportunities being offered to help couples take new growth steps in their marriages.

Pastors should never forget that they are always sending signals to their parishioners, signals that will be the basis on which a parishioner makes the decision in the parking lot whether or not even to mention the slightest suggestion of marital problems at home. Consciously and unconsciously parishioners evaluate a pastor's care and counseling skills with such questions as: Will my pastor understand? Will my pastor be able to listen without judging me? Does my pastor even care about our marriage and family? Will our pastor know how to respond and know what to do about our marriage problems?

Pastors should not be surprised to learn that they are communicating answers to their parishioners' questions by the sermons they preach, the prayers they offer, and their approach to people in pastoral conversations and pastoral care opportunities. Parishioners will especially gauge a pastor's receptivity to their personal and relationship pain by the pastor's own ability to step out from behind a professional religious facade and appropriately share his or her own vulnerabilities and struggles. Pastors who can affirm their humanness while at the same time maintaining their essential professional role and boundaries will greatly assist parishioners who want to take the risky step of acknowledging somehow to their pastor that all is not well at home.

Howard Clinebell offers practical help for how a church can develop a responsive ministry to married couples, with caring and educational attention to such areas as preparation for marriage, support for new marriages, enrichment for young parents and for mid-years' marriages, preparation for creative retirement, spiritual and values enhancement for marriages, and enhancing sexuality. Clinebell's four-step strategy will aid many churches to develop or expand their ministry to couples: (1) assigning responsibilities to a "Marriage and Family Wholeness Committee" that works in partnership with the pastor to develop ministry and educational programs; (2) sizing up and prioritizing the needs in the congregation and the community; (3) devising goals, strategies, and a workable plan to respond to unmet needs; and (4) implementing the plan and deciding on the next steps to meet other needs of couples and families.[5] When clergy and their churches devise and implement creative educational and supportive programs for couples and families, they offer a valuable ministry that enhances marriage growth for most couples while making it more likely that troubled couples will recognize their need for help and seek their pastor as their first choice for professional help. Creating a vital educational and supportive context of pastoral care to marriages will set the stage for increased opportunities for the first-stage invitation to marriage counseling.

The Pastoral Invitation

This first step in the five-stage counseling model can take any one of several forms. Sometimes the invitation is a matter of the pastor responding to a couple's request for help in person or over the telephone. Then the invitation is more just a matter of recording a date on the pastor's calendar for the first meeting in the pastor's office, with no attempt to begin any marriage counseling at that point.

More often, the invitation to couple counseling is likely to occur during or following a pastoral contact on other matters. For example, Pastor Pamela Smith made a call to the home of Paul and Gloria Sampson to discuss the baptism next Sunday of the Sampsons' infant daughter. While Pastor Smith was explaining the meaning of the baptism for them and their daughter, the conversation also led to other concerns for the Sampsons. Gloria explained that she was spending a lot of time at her parents' home nearby because of her mother's failing health and her father's full-time devotion to the family business. In the meantime, Paul had been threatened with losing his job because the accounting firm he works for had lost several major clients. In the midst of all this conversation, it became increasingly clear to Pastor Smith that Paul and Gloria were under so much stress that it could be affecting their marriage.

> Pastor: As we're talking I'm concerned about the heavy pressures you are both feeling these days. I'm wondering if all that stress ever makes it hard for you to get along with each other without becoming impatient or edgy.

Gloria: Frankly, Pastor, I *am* worried about that. Just in the last month I've been feeling an uncomfortable distance beginning to come between Paul and me.

Paul: Sometimes when I come home from work I just don't feel like talking, and it seems those are always the times Gloria gets after me with a lot of questions. I'm sorry, but it's really annoying.

Pastor: Right now you're both involved with plans for the baptism next Sunday, and you have company coming from out of town for the weekend. But after everyone has gone home, I'd like us to meet in my office so we can talk some more about how things are going with your relationship in the midst of so many difficult pressures. Would you both be willing to do that?

Paul: Gloria, if you're willing, I think I am. Maybe it would be a help to talk some more about how all that is going on right now is affecting our marriage.

Gloria: These aren't easy things to talk about, but I'm willing. Sometimes I get worried about where we might be heading.

Because the marital crisis was not overwhelming or incapacitating and the Sampsons were effectively focused on the approaching baptism, Pastor Smith resumed talking about the final details for the baptism without attempting any marriage counseling. Before leaving, Pastor Smith set an appointment in the next week for meeting Paul and Gloria in her office at the church.

Pastor Smith's invitation to marriage counseling grew out of alert and empathetic pastoral listening. Occasions for making a similar invitation occur in many church-related settings. The pastor who listens carefully at meetings or in the course of routine pastoral calling will often hear clues that a marriage is under extraordinary stress. At the right moment in a private conversation with one or both partners, a concerned pastor can invite the couple to come together to the pastor's office so the three of them can explore how the relationship might be helped.

Of course, there may be occasions when a pastor offers such an invitation to a couple and one or both persons say no. Some pastors may hesitate to take that risk, even being concerned that they might jeopardize their pastoral relationship with the couple by suggesting that they might have a "bad marriage." However, if the pastor's intention is simply to offer an invitation and not to render a judgment, then the pastor has taken an appropriate and responsible risk. Indeed, not to offer such an invitation could be considered doing the couple a disservice. Even if the couple does say no, the pastor has expressed concern for them and indicated a willingness to talk with them about their marriage in the future if and when they are persuaded that it is time to talk with their pastor.

Pastors know that it is not uncommon for husbands or wives to come alone to see the pastor so they can talk about their marriage and their disappointments and frustrations over what they perceive as their spouse's failures. Jill Kline's conversation with Pastor Michael Bates in his office after she had just helped the secretary fold next Sunday's bulletins will be familiar to most pastors.

> Jill: I don't know how long I can go on like this! Ever since Stan got this new job, he might as well never come home. He takes no responsibility around the house or with the kids. In fact, when he is home I feel like I've just got one more child to take care of, and I sure don't need that! What I need is a responsible, grown-up husband.

> Pastor: Jill, you're tired of things the way they are between you and Stan since he got this new job, and you feel things can't go on any longer the way they are now. However, you and I cannot change what's going on without Stan's help. I would really like to see you both together. As soon as possible, let's arrange a time that will be convenient for the three of us to meet here in my office.

> Jill: I suppose you're right, but I'd be surprised if Stan will bother to come. He doesn't do anything anymore that I want him to do.

> Pastor: Will you ask him? Tell him that you spoke to me today and that I said it is important for him to come with you so we can all talk together about your relationship.

There should be no surprise when a parishioner expresses reservations about the pastor's invitation for both spouses to come together to the pastor's office. It is not an uncommon occurrence for a person to reply, "Pastor, I would really like to come with Joe to talk with you, but three years ago we went once to a marriage counselor, and he said that he would never go back again to a marriage counselor even if the counseling were free! I know he won't come. Once Joe makes up his mind, there's no changing him. You know how stubborn he can be."

Despite the parishioner's convictions about her husband, the pastor should be careful not to make any assumptions. The pastor still does not know whether or not Joe will come this time with his wife to the pastor's office. All that is clear is that Joe's wife thinks that Joe will not come. Either of two pastoral responses can be made.

> Pastor: Your husband has been very reluctant in the past to have anything to do with marriage counseling. When you talk with him, tell him that I have invited both of you because it is important for him to be involved with you for the improvement of your marriage.

Or the pastor may go further:

> Pastor: Your husband has said in the past that he was not going to any more marriage counseling. With your permission I will call him and tell him that you have talked with me about some of your concerns for your marriage. I will invite him to come with you to my office so the three of us can talk together about your relationship.

Sometimes the second spouse will request an individual session with the pastor before coming as a couple. The second spouse can easily imagine that the pastor has already formed an opinion in favor of the first spouse. The second spouse may feel that it is necessary to have equal time with the pastor before the first session of couple counseling. The pastor should minimize the extent of what was heard from the first spouse and make every effort to decline seeing the second spouse alone. Seeing the second spouse in an individual session before seeing the couple together will only delay the start of effective marriage counseling and possibly get the pastor caught between the two spouses, because they are only left to imagine the worst about what each is telling the pastor about the other.

If the pastor feels that there is no option but to grant an insistent request from the second spouse for a preliminary individual session, marriage counseling is not yet the main goal for the pastor in that session. The principal objective for the pastor in that situation will be to communicate concern and understanding for both partners without taking sides, and then to offer once again the invitation for both of them to come together to the pastor's office. In this first stage, the pastor's main intention is to offer an invitation that both partners will accept for both of them to meet together with the pastor.

A spouse may also turn down the pastor's invitation because of confused or ambivalent feelings toward the marriage that need to be clarified before couple counseling can even be considered. As a rule, marriage counseling will not be productive if one partner has serious reservations about wanting to continue the marriage or to work on the relationship. Successful marriage counseling requires at least a mutual agreement that each spouse wants a better marital relationship. When persons express serious feelings of reservation or confusion about their commitment to the marriage, the pastor can make one of two invitations to the husband or wife.

> Pastor: You are not at all certain that you still love your wife, and you need time to think about your commitment to her before you can even consider coming to counseling with her. I'll be glad to help you sort through those feelings. However, if more than two individual sessions with me are needed for you, I will then recommend that you and your wife go to another counselor for couple counseling. It would not be fair to your wife for me to do extended counseling with you and then attempt to be an unbiased counselor for both of you as a couple.

Or the pastor may suggest the opposite plan.

> Pastor: Because I am the pastor for both of you, it is important that I work with you and your spouse from as neutral a perspective as possible. If I become your individual counselor, I would no longer be in a neutral position with respect to both of you. So I recommend that you do your individual counseling with another counselor, and then if and when you feel committed to work on your marriage I will be more than glad to see both of you together, if that is what you both would like.

It is important that a pastor not become confused about when and whether to do individual and couple counseling with one or both spouses. As a rule, couple counseling and extended individual counseling with one or both spouses should *not* be done at the same time by the pastor. Nor should a pastor work with a couple if the pastor has done extended counseling earlier with one of the spouses. *Unless both spouses feel that the pastor is as much their own counselor as their partner's counselor, the success of the marriage counseling will be in jeopardy as soon as it begins.*

There are pastors who may feel that it is preferable, as a matter of routine, to begin marriage counseling by seeing both spouses separately from the outset. Some counselors make the case that both partners may find it easier to talk to the pastor without the other spouse being present, and that likewise it will be easier, presumably, for the pastor if the two spouses are not fighting with each other in the first session. However, the disadvantages of such a procedure nearly always far outweigh the supposed advantages. Invariably, both husband and wife will be suspicious about what the pastor has been told individually before both come for counseling together. They each will be concerned that the pastor is going to be biased in favor of the other spouse right from the beginning. For marriage counseling to have any chance of being helpful, it is essential at the outset of the counseling that both spouses know what the other has told the pastor about their marital differences. Obviously, this requires that both spouses be present to hear what the other has to say. When that procedure occurs right from the beginning, neither spouse is as likely to think that the other has an unfair advantage. If either the husband or the wife begins to feel that the counseling process is unfair or that the pastor is no longer impartial, the counseling will have little hope of success.

Finally, if the pastor begins by seeing each partner separately for marriage counseling, it is more likely that the pastor will be seen as a judge who is to decide which spouse is right and which is wrong, having begun by hearing both partners' stories separately. But, it is not the pastor's job to be a judge, and the pastor cannot be an effective counselor if she or he is perceived by either spouse to be in that role. The pastor's intent to be equally concerned and unbiased toward both spouses is best ensured by inviting them to begin the marriage counseling process together.

The Initial Session with the Couple

Pastor Barbara Cowan is successful in bringing Ron and Mary Nelson to the second stage of the counseling plan when they agree to see her together in her office for the first time. There are five important tasks for Pastor Cowan to accomplish before she welcomes the Nelsons to her office, however. First, she will have inquired from an attorney or a state or county agency what, if any, responsibilities she as a pastor has if in the course of pastoral counseling she learns of the physical or sexual abuse of a vulnerable adult or child. A call to the state attorney general's office or to the county or local office for child protection and vulnerable adult protection should clarify what the law expects of her as a pastor. Pastor Cowan wants to know what legal requirements she may need to observe, because she knows that even in the course of marriage counseling she could learn about child or vulnerable adult abuse. Second, Pastor Cowan will have to research the viable community and area resources where she can refer parishioners for drug and alcohol abuse, for domestic abuse shelter and treatment, and for counseling and psychotherapy. She will pick up professional brochures and business cards that she can give to her parishioners to facilitate a referral. Third, she will make herself familiar with Possible Critical Issues in the First Session (appendix C). She then will make a copy for her quick reference during the counseling session. Fourth, she will also prepare a copy of The Six Steps of the First Session with Approximate Times (see page 50). Fifth, she will make two copies each of the Covenant for Pastoral Marriage Counseling and the Pastoral Marriage Counseling Questionnaire. Pastor Cowan will have all of these forms and the referral brochures and business cards with her during the meeting with the couple. It is essential that Pastor Cowan have carefully reviewed these aids and forms before the first meeting with the Nelsons. Then these materials will be much more helpful as she makes reference to them during the counseling session.

The Covenant for Pastoral Marriage Counseling

Because most counselees have misconceptions and misunderstandings about marriage counseling, much time and energy can be wasted throughout the process as counselees and counselor deal with their often conflicting notions about what should be happening in the course of the counseling. To deal with this problem, the Covenant for Pastoral Marriage Counseling offers a defining statement to the counselees and the pastor for engaging in pastoral marriage counseling.

Equally significant if not of greater concern for a counselor is the fact that most all spouses enter marriage counseling from an adversarial point of view toward each other. Human nature being what it is, particularly in such an intimate relationship as marriage with high expectations for need-fulfillment, spouses seem naturally and quickly to blame each other when needs and expectations go unfulfilled. Not surprisingly, spouses respond defensively to protect themselves from the blaming and the attacks that come from the other. At its worst, marriage counseling can quickly deteriorate into an emotional and verbal boxing match, with the pastor left to function as the referee and as the moral judge who is to render a decision about who is right and who is wrong. It is no wonder many pastors and parishioners have decided that they want nothing to do with such a potentially destructive counseling process that might easily leave a couple with even more marital stress and pain than they had before beginning the counseling.

The Covenant for Pastoral Marriage Counseling (CPMC) is a very important form that the pastor introduces to the couple in the first counseling session.[6] The purpose of the CPMC is to define a positive pastoral counseling process with the most promising potential for marital understanding, reconciliation, and growth. Perhaps the greatest significance of the CPMC is that it is an instrument for turning the spouses from defensive marital adversaries into cooperative marital partners who can work together to resolve their relationship issues. The CPMC sets the stage, as a framework of mutual understanding and agreement, for a caring and respectful pastoral dialogical process offering a genuine promise for reconciliation and hope for troubled couples. Finally, the CPMC states the three options for the final counseling session so that the couple clearly knows what is going to happen in the counseling process, including the possibility of an early referral. If the couple agrees to the CPMC, they sign two copies of the covenant, one copy for them and one copy for the pastor.

The CPMC Defines a Context That Facilitates Dialogue for Individual and Relationship Growth

The counseling pastor should understand and be able to interpret the purpose of each of the ten points in the CPMC.

1. Marriage counseling is a process, both within the pastor's office and outside the counseling sessions, for learning and gaining understanding about oneself, one's partner, and the marriage. Indeed, counseling is an exciting opportunity for the spouses to learn more together about themselves and their relationship.
2. The purpose of marriage counseling is *not* for the pastor to speak authoritatively to people about what they should do about their relationship problems. Indeed, regardless of what the pastor says, both spouses will make up their own minds, and they will make their own decisions. The aim of the counseling process is to help them make the best decisions for themselves, their marriage, and their family.

3. For the sake of honesty it is essential that spouses understand that pastoral marriage counseling does not guarantee certain results. Pastoral short-term counseling is a structured process that is largely dependent upon the motivation and the commitment of the two spouses to work together for reconciliation and a more fulfilling marriage.

4. Attempting to change someone else is a futile undertaking. But when spouses shift their attention to changing their own behavior instead of their spouse's, remarkable progress can begin to be made for the better in the relationship.

5. There are many people who have the mistaken notion that the best use of counseling is to spend the time complaining about one's spouse's behavior. Such complaining accomplishes nothing, while magnificently deflecting attention from the only person the complainer can change, namely, herself or himself.

6. Many couples find their way to marriage counseling because they only know how to fight and attack each other. The purpose of counseling is to help couples find better, relationship-building ways to communicate and resolve their differences.

7. The pastor will certainly feel each spouse, however subtly, wanting the pastor to take sides, to say how "obviously" wrong the other spouse is. Many couples are in conflict exactly because both spouses are so intent upon proving they are right and the other is wrong. Such efforts at promoting one's own self-rightness invariably lead to the worsening of marital strife.

8. It is not unusual for spouses, assuming the role of psychologist, to be sure that the marriage would be a lot better if the other spouse undertook some self-improvement with the help of the counselor. The hope is that the counselor will be as psychologically astute as the spouse, and recognize and provide all the help and assistance the other spouse needs for adequate improvement in such areas as self-esteem, procrastination, commitment, responsibility, and punctuality, not to mention other such "character flaws" as failing to pick up after oneself and not putting one's dirty dishes in the dishwasher.

9. In a similar vein, many spouses in conflict will be certain that the marriage problems are due to the other spouse having a serious mental or personality disorder. It is important from the outset to disabuse spouses of any notion that their pastor will be attempting to determine which spouse has the greater or lesser mental health. The primary issue for the counseling is the relative health and well-being of the *marriage*. If, indeed, there are any genuine mental health issues related

to one or the other spouse, those issues are to be dealt with within the larger purpose of both spouses working together for the improvement of their marriage.

10. The question in the counseling is how well the marital relationship is working to fulfill each spouse's hopes and needs, and what each spouse will change about his or her own behavior for the sake of improving the marriage.

These ten understandings and guidelines define the most promising counseling context for a hopeful and productive dialogue between two partners who want a more loving and fulfilling relationship.

Two sentences near the end of the CPMC state that marriage counseling will not be useful if either spouse is presently involved in an extramarital romantic and/or sexual relationship. Unless there is a sole commitment by both spouses to the marriage, the counseling process will be little more than the further covering of deceit.

The Setting for Pastoral Marriage Counseling

Another necessary step for Pastor Cowan is to ensure that she has an appropriate and confidential setting for meeting with the Nelsons. Unless extraordinary circumstances require other arrangements, pastoral marriage counseling will ordinarily occur in the pastor's office, not in the couple's home. Marriage counseling is best done in a setting where privacy and confidentiality can be assured, and where there is little likelihood of interruption at the door or by the telephone. In the pastor's office the pastor obviously has the greatest control over the physical arrangement of the furniture and the limiting of disturbing distractions.

Here it must be emphasized that the purpose of pastoral marriage counseling is to facilitate a promising dialogue between husband and wife so their own words can take on new meaning for the renewal of their relationship. Pastoral marriage counseling also, by its very nature, involves the pastor in that dialogue so that the candor and honesty of the pastor's words can encourage a truthful and open exchange between husband and wife. This encounter of honest and genuine words within God's loving presence brings marital conflict and alienation once again to the hopeful possibility for reconciliation.

Such a theology of dialogic encounter for pastoral marriage counseling suggests a physical setting of three chairs, equally distant from each other, and arranged with no obstacle between them so that each person can see the other two with equal ease. There should not be a desk between the pastor and the couple, and it is always much better if the husband and wife are not seated side by side on a couch facing the pastor. If they are seated together on a couch, their own direct conversation, which is highly desirable, will be awkward and less natural, and they are more likely to talk to each other through the pastor instead of speaking directly to each other.

A box of tissues should be unobtrusively within reach. The absence of ashtrays will indicate that no smoking is expected. A small clock may be set on a table in plain view of everyone so that the realistic limitations of time are always present. The pastor can say, "Let's do all we can in the next fifty minutes and then make plans for the next session." Such a comment at the beginning of the session will signal to the couple that there is a time to begin and a time to end, so everyone's attention can focus more promptly on the couple's main concerns and issues.

The pastor may wish to have a pad for recording notes during the session. Note taking is certainly appropriate as long as it does not become an obvious block to communication or a distraction to the couple's concentration. If notes from counseling sessions are saved for future reference by the pastor, it is essential that some provision be made for keeping them in a securely locked file cabinet. Pastors are discouraged from keeping a file of counseling notes and papers after the counseling has ended. Pastors should assure their counselees that everything written by the counselees will be returned to them, and all other notes and records will be destroyed by the pastor immediately upon the conclusion of the planned counseling sessions.

The Counseling Process in the First Session

Pastor Barbara Cowan follows six steps as she takes Ron and Mary Nelson through the initial counseling session (see the summary table of the six steps on page 50). The first step is *welcoming* the couple to the pastor's office and the counseling process. Pastor Cowan extends a warm greeting to her parishioners and thanks them for coming to the session. After showing them the chairs where they are to sit, she summarizes the events that have led to this meeting. She explains that after hearing Mary's brief comments following the church meeting, she felt that it would be good for the three of them to talk together. Pastor Cowan may also say that she has a plan for the couple that she will explain later. It is also important for her to mention that they should be able to do all that they can accomplish in this meeting in an hour. She might offer statements such as:

"Hi, Mary. Hi, Ron. I'm glad to see you. Thanks for coming tonight."

"I was talking with Mary, and because your marriage is about both of you I thought it would be best for the three of us to talk together."

"Also, I told Mary that I have a plan, and I want to get to that plan a little later."

"I think we should be able to do all that we can do in fifty minutes or an hour."

The second step is one of *structured listening* as each of the spouses has a turn to explain the marital problems or tensions as she or he perceives and understands those issues. This period is structured by the pastor's intention to listen carefully to each spouse. There should be little or no exchange at this time between the spouses. If one spouse tries to interrupt or debate with the one speaking, the pastor should gently but firmly say that the other spouse will also have an opportunity to address the marital problems without interruption.

Pastor Cowan introduces the structured listening by saying, "I would like us to begin with each of you explaining what you think are the troubling or stressful issues in your relationship. I assume that there will be some issues that you each see quite differently from the other. Who would like to begin?" She does not appoint or designate a beginner.

Pastor Cowan listens only for understanding, and may ask questions for clarification while using brief summary statements to communicate understanding. This is not a time for her to attempt to solve problems or to offer facile solutions. It is important that each spouse feels heard and taken seriously by Pastor Cowan. After being sure to hear all that the first spouse wants to say, her full attention is directed to the second spouse. This structured listening step may last approximately twenty to twenty-five minutes. In some instances, for the sake of time, a pastor may need to be direct about saying to counselees that the pastor needs an overview more than exact details of marital complaints. The pastor can say that there will be an opportunity in a later session for examining all the details.

Pastor Cowan may permit some limited respectful exchanges between the spouses if they occur during this stage of structured listening. However, the main purpose of this stage is for each spouse to have the opportunity to explain his or her point of view regarding the marriage problems without interruption or argument from the other spouse.

The third step is a *realistic summary and affirmation* by Pastor Cowan of the seriousness of the various marital issues as just presented by both spouses. It is very important in this summarizing statement that she accurately reflect back the level of stress and pain felt by each spouse over the conflicts and tensions in the marriage. There should be no attempt by Pastor Cowan to diminish the level of stress that each spouse is feeling, or to suggest that the marital problems are typical for their stage of marriage and will therefore pass in time. If the spouses do not feel that she has a fairly accurate understanding of how they see their marriage problems, they may well conclude that she cannot be of much help to them.

In response to the issues troubling the couple, the fourth step is for Pastor Cowan *to offer a hopeful and productive plan* for the couple to take positive steps to work together for a better and more fulfilling marriage. The plan offered by Pastor Cowan is for a specific number of counseling sessions, individual and together, that will involve both persons completing a questionnaire about themselves and about their relationship. She explains that, after completing the questionnaire, she will see each spouse individually for one or two sessions. Then she will see them together again two times. At the second of these, the final session, there will be three specific options: the termination of counseling, referral to another professional resource, or no more than two or three follow-up sessions for the couple with the pastor. Pastor Cowan emphasizes that this proposed plan has a designated ending point and goes for a brief number of sessions, but that it also will provide the opportunity for the couple to take a good, thorough look at the many aspects of their marriage so they will have a better understanding of the issues they need to work on or resolve. She explains that by the final session the couple will be able to make better informed decisions about the next steps to take for themselves, for their marriage, and for their family. She introduces the counseling plan this way:

> Pastor: I have a plan for you to consider. I am very concerned for both of you and your marriage. This plan I want to offer you is the best way for me to be of help over a brief number of sessions. The plan is for me next to see each of you separately once or twice, and I would give you some homework to complete before I would see you. Then after one or two individual sessions with each of you, the three of us would meet for two more sessions. At the final session there would be three options for us to consider: first, we could decide that no more counseling is necessary; second, I could refer you to another professional counseling resource in the community; third, we could decide that you will see me together for another one to three sessions, but no more than that.

Along with the outline of the short-term counseling plan, Pastor Cowan defines what pastoral marriage counseling is and how it works. In her best words, she summarizes the ten points in the CPMC. Pastor Cowan won't remember all of the points, and therefore it is appropriate at this juncture in the conversation for her to hand a copy of the CPMC to the husband and wife.

> Pastor: I'm enthusiastic about this plan, because it will help you to sort out and look closely at the issues in your relationship. And you will be working together in a positive way on your marriage. This Covenant for Pastoral Marriage Counseling explains everything that will be involved in this promising counseling process.

She then allows time for each of them quietly to read the full CPMC statement. When they have finished reading the statement, she asks if there are any questions. Then she inquires, "Is this plan what you would like to do together?" If the couple is ready to continue with the counseling plan, they sign two copies of the CPMC. The couple keeps one copy, and Pastor Cowan retains the other copy. She then may affirm the couple by saying, "You have just taken a very important step in agreeing that you want to work together for the improvement of your marriage!"

Pastor Cowan now moves promptly to the fifth step of *handing a copy of the PMCQ to each spouse*. Pastor Cowan acknowledges that the questionnaire possibly may take each of them an hour or more to complete. However, she adds that most people who complete the questionnaire find it to be helpful to them in better understanding their marriage. She also encourages the couple to use additional sheets for responding to the questions that will require longer answers.

Pastor Cowan then makes a special and important request that the spouses not share with each other their completed questionnaires. Furthermore, she may reassure the couple that their responses on the questionnaire are only for her to read and discuss with the writer, but not to pass on to the other spouse.

> Pastor: I am asking you not to share your completed questionnaires with each other. What you write will be only for me to read. And I won't be discussing anything you write with the other person. What you write is just for me and our discussion in the individual session.

Then she makes arrangements for the completed questionnaires to be returned to her at least two days before the individual sessions so there is time for her to read them.

It is possible that a pastor will encounter a couple in which one or both persons say that it will be difficult for them to write down their responses to the items in the PMCQ. Because of a lack of sufficient education or for other personal reasons a counselee may refuse the request to give written responses to the questionnaire. The information sought on the questionnaire is important and essential, but answering the questionnaire should not become a test of wills between the pastor and the parishioner. Instead, the pastor has some alternative options to offer without compromising the value of the information sought by the questionnaire.

One option is for the pastor to explain that the counselee may take the questionnaire home, read it over, and write just a word or a couple of words for each question. These responses would then be discussed more fully with the pastor. Another option would be for the counselee to read the questionnaire, consider his or her answers, and write nothing. The questionnaire would then be discussed in full with the pastor. If the parishioner claims to be unable to read the questionnaire at all, then the pastor can explain that in the individual session the pastor will read each question to the parishioner as the basis for the interview.

In the highly unlikely event that a parishioner outright refuses to have anything to do with the questionnaire, the pastor should listen carefully to the counselee's objection while also reviewing again with the counselee the CPMC, which the counselee has just signed. The CPMC states that the questionnaire will be part of the process. If one of the spouses does not want to be forthcoming with any information such as that sought by the questionnaire, then the marriage counseling process cannot proceed. The pastor should propose either a referral to a community counseling resource or postponement of the marriage counseling with the pastor until both feel ready to undertake the process together.

Finally, Pastor Cowan in the sixth step *brings the counseling session to a close*. Once again she can affirm the couple with words such as: "You have taken a very important step, deciding to work together on your marriage. I will look forward to reading your questionnaires and seeing you each in a week or two." Arrangements are made at this point for the counseling sessions with each spouse. The sessions may be scheduled at each person's convenience. Spouses may be seen a week apart, or they may both be seen the same day or evening. Most important is that the spouses have time to finish the questionnaires and return them to Pastor Cowan two days in advance so she has time to read them before the individual counseling sessions. She then may offer a prayer for God's care, guidance, and loving presence to be with the couple and with their family as both of them make important decisions for their marriage.

The Six Steps of the First Session with Approximate Times

1. The welcome (4 minutes)
2. Structured listening (25 minutes)
3. Realistic summary and affirmation (5 minutes)
4. The pastor offers a hopeful and productive plan with the Covenant for Pastoral Marriage Counseling (7 minutes)
5. The pastor gives a copy of the Pastoral Marriage Counseling Questionnaire to each spouse (3 minutes)
6. The close of the session (6 minutes)

Clearly, the first session is structured so several necessary steps can be covered. But pastors may wonder, "What if the counselees don't cooperate, with one or both of them insisting upon using most or all of the time to talk about their complaints about the marriage?" This structured counseling plan requires the pastor to be an active guide through the process. Timidity or passivity on the part of the pastor will make it impossible for the counseling plan to be accomplished. Most all couples will welcome and be reassured by the pastor's confident counseling leadership. If a couple refuses to cooperate and follow the pastor's guidance through the process, this may be a clear indication that an immediate referral to a professional marriage counselor will be best for the couple.

Checklist for an Effective First Pastoral Marriage Counseling Session

The initial counseling session should ordinarily flow naturally through the six steps, particularly as the pastor keeps in mind that the purpose of the session is not to solve complex marital problems but to get the couple started in a hope-filled and promising process that will facilitate their working together on their relationship challenges. As the pastor leads the couple through the six steps, the presence or occurrence of seven important themes will add significantly to the effectiveness of the session for helping the couple.

1. Meeting in their pastor's office in a structured counseling session provides an important safe setting within which negative and destructive patterns of marital communication are interrupted. In the presence of a respected third person who represents ecclesiastical authority and important faith values, both spouses should feel sufficiently secure so they can risk the kind of open discussion necessary for healing to begin in their marriage.

2. Such a secure counseling setting is ensured as the pastor communicates verbally and nonverbally that the conversation will be respectful and productive, particularly as the pastor discourages interrupting or arguing. Often, essential ground rules for clear communication can be simply demonstrated if the pastor refuses to respond to an interrupting spouse and continues to direct attention to the spouse who is still talking. Or the pastor may say:

> Pastor: It is important that both of you be able to speak without interruption so I can fully understand what each of you wants to say. It is best if you talk about yourself and your own feelings and experiences and refrain from describing or characterizing the other person.

3. It cannot be overstated how important it is for the spouses to hear each other explain to the pastor the problems in the marriage as they each see them. Indeed, a common cause of much marital conflict is that spouses really have not fully heard what concerns each other. But, by being with their pastor in an optimal setting for speaking, listening, and understanding, the chances are much greater that the spouses will hear more thoroughly and more extensively than before the full extent of concern and pain felt by each other. This depth of mutual hearing and learning cannot possibly be achieved if the spouses are seen initially separately by the pastor.

4. Furthermore, after each spouse has voiced concerns and distress about the marriage, it can be very helpful for the pastor to inquire about the level of commitment of each spouse to the marriage and to the counseling process. If one or both spouses have ambivalent or confused feelings, it is good for that ambivalence and confusion to be put out in the open at the outset so there are no illusions about the amount of healing that needs to be accomplished in the marriage. The question by the pastor to the couple, "Do you still want to be married to each other?" can elicit a very helpful response and assessment from each spouse. The more enthusiastic and positive the response is from each spouse, the more likely

the couple will be successful in working through and resolving their marriage problems, no matter how severe those conflicts may be.

5. Pastors doing marriage counseling will be all the more helpful if they are skilled in using reflecting summary statements. The instinctive reaction for many pastors will be to talk "at" and to talk "past" their counselees without carefully and convincingly demonstrating first that they really have heard the words and the feelings being expressed. Effective listening, most often conveyed through periodic summary statements, can greatly help parishioners to explain and describe their concerns, and also to give permission and encouragement to a counselee to continue with more detail and self-revelation. Pastors should listen for the best proof that they have heard and understood their counselees, such as when the counselee says in so many words, "You got it! That's exactly what bothers me!"

> Christa: Martin's mother is a wonderful person, but I'm tired of the way she is always intruding in our marriage. She's got advice on everything, how to raise the kids, how to decorate our house, where we should go on vacation, and now she thinks I should quit my job so I can stay home all day with the kids and cook meals for her son. I'm tired of listening to her, and I think it's time that Martin showed some backbone and let his mother know that he's on my side because I'm his wife!

> Pastor: Christa, even though you respect your mother-in-law as a person, you are upset about all the ways she gets herself involved in your marriage and family, especially around decisions you and Martin should make on your own without her being in the middle of your family life. You're particularly bothered because Martin hasn't told his mother to mind her own business and to leave the running of your home and family to him and you.

> Christa: That's it exactly! And if Martin isn't going to tell his mother, then I'm going to do it myself!

The pastor's summary of Christa's stated concerns does not mean that the pastor agrees with Christa's characterization of her husband. If either Christa or Martin feels that the pastor has shown some bias in the summary statement, the pastor can clarify that misunderstanding.

6. In the first session and throughout the marriage counseling process, the pastor should always be looking for legitimate ways to link the couple by drawing their attention to experiences, views, or feelings they hold in

common, even if they are negative experiences or feelings. Such linking may in some cases bring a husband and wife to see that they have more in common than the painful and divisive differences absorbing so much of their current attention and energy. However, any attempts to link a couple should not be done in such a way as to imply that their differences are insignificant or not to be taken seriously. But drawing attention to genuine concerns or feelings that both spouses share in common may help to set their differences in such a context of "common ground" that they may see new possibilities for resolving the conflicts that are separating them.

> Pastor: Marilyn and Ray, you both described different problem areas in your marriage, and you don't agree on what the main cause of tension and conflict between you is. However, you both said that the first eight years of your marriage were good years, and you agree that the problems between you didn't start until you moved here to Centerville. You both also said that you are concerned about how your marital problems are affecting your children. In your own ways, I think you are both very troubled by your conflicts and by your inability so far to find a satisfactory way out of your problems toward a more loving relationship. You really disagree on some very important issues, but I thought I was also hearing these important similarities between you in what both of you have been saying.

7. A pastor has a responsibility consistently to lift up a hope grounded in reality. Most often the hope will be for reconciliation and healing in a marriage. Sometimes the hope will be for the possibility that fractured lives may make a new beginning without each other after a divorce. Hope is always present in the Christian faith regardless of the circumstances, and a caring pastor will faithfully point to that hope. But hope is always honest. A wise pastor will resist any urge to be overly reassuring. If couples are offered a reassurance that does not seem like it takes seriously the depth or extent of their problems, they may rightly assume that their pastor does not really understand the full extent of their marital distress. Likewise, the caring pastor will not use prayer to minimize the reality of marriage and relationship brokenness. Pain and alienation can be fully acknowledged in the same prayer affirming God's loving presence that is always in the midst of every human struggle, a faithful presence that sustains, that offers guidance, and that even offers hope for promising new directions not yet envisioned or dared.

> ### *Seven Themes Checklist for an Effective First Counseling Session*
>
> 1. Spouses meet with the pastor in the pastor's office.
> 2. A conversation respectful of both spouses is emphasized.
> 3. Spouses hear each other's concerns about the marriage.
> 4. The pastor inquires about each spouse's level of commitment to the marriage.
> 5. The pastor uses reflecting summary statements with each spouse.
> 6. The pastor links the couple's common concerns and interests.
> 7. The pastor offers the couple hope grounded in reality.

When All Doesn't Go as Planned and Other Critical Counseling Issues

As she talked with the Nelsons, Pastor Cowan held a copy of Possible Critical Issues in the First Session (PCIFS) in her lap (see appendix C). She had reviewed and carefully thought through these several issues, so she felt that she was ready to offer an appropriate pastoral response should any of those critical issues arise. The PCIFS form in her lap could be a helpful reference should she need it. The critical issues requiring an immediate pastoral response will include (1) a concern by either spouse that the other is currently or has been involved in an affair, (2) alcohol or chemical abuse by either spouse, (3) physical or sexual abuse reported by either spouse,[7] (4) obvious mental health issues, (5) compulsive gambling or sexual behavior reported as a disturbing issue, (6) a desire by one or both spouses not to proceed with the marriage counseling plan, and (7) one or both spouses not having the education or verbal skills to complete the Pastoral Marriage Counseling Questionnaire.

Important counseling issues for helping couples will be discussed more fully in chapter 5. Once pastors have given these issues thought and reflection, with the assistance of the PCIFS form readily at hand in the first session, pastors will be able to exercise good judgment as they guide spouses in dealing with these issues that can be quite troubling for couples.

Conclusion

Pastor Cowan offered a plan for Ron and Mary Nelson to begin working together toward a more fulfilling marriage with fewer areas for misunderstanding and tension. The plan has been put into action for Ron and Mary to engage in a process that will help them to begin taking a careful and thorough look at themselves and at their marriage. Pastor Cowan is trusting that with God's presence and help Ron and Mary will make good decisions about the changes they will make for a stronger and more loving marriage. What Pastor Cowan has accomplished in this first session is perhaps well summarized by Charles Stewart's observation that instead of giving advice and directions, a pastor is ". . . *for* the individuals, for their right to choose their own destiny under God, and for the possibility of there coming creative solutions out of discreative situations."[8] With that lively hope of finding creative alternatives to a stressed or broken relationship, Pastor Cowan will now continue with the counseling plan and see Ron and Mary individually.

Chapter Three

The Plan for Meeting
with Each Spouse

An essential art in being married is knowing how to be an individual in the union without being so individualized that the union is characterized by two persons living parallel and non-intersecting existences—and conversely, knowing how to be a vital couple without being so fused and enmeshed that the essential individuality of each person is lost.

> —Robert W. Wohlfort, "Marriage in the Second
> Half of Life," in *Handbook for Basic Types of
> Pastoral Care and Counseling*, edited by
> Howard W. Stone and William M. Clements

This chapter covers:

~ A four-step counseling process
~ Analyzing the questionnaires
~ The exploratory interview
~ An outline for individual sessions
~ Six key questions
~ Arranging the room
~ Reflecting on the data

After church the next Sunday, Ron and Mary Nelson handed Pastor Barbara Cowan separate envelopes containing their completed questionnaires. They each smiled as they assured their pastor that they had not read the other's completed questionnaire, just as she had requested. Pastor Cowan then confirmed again the appointment times for each individual counseling session. The Nelsons had said that it would work best for both of them to see Pastor Cowan the same evening, about ten days after the first counseling session. Ron's schedule worked best for him to come to Pastor Cowan's office at 7:15 p.m. Mary would come at 8:30 p.m., allowing Pastor Cowan about ten minutes to put Ron's papers back in a folder and to take another look through Mary's completed questionnaire before meeting with her.

As Pastor Cowan was driving home from church, she was puzzled about why she could see each of the Nelsons separately now, whereas she was strongly urged not to see Ron and Mary separately to begin the counseling. What, she wondered, was different now about these individual sessions? Why wouldn't there be problems similar to the difficulties likely to occur when both spouses are seen separately at the outset? Why won't the spouses feel suspicious that they are being criticized and put in a bad light by the other spouse? And if their pastor sees one partner twice but the other partner only once, why won't it appear that their pastor has taken sides?

The truth is that both the husband and the wife might very well be suspicious about what occurs when their partner is talking with the pastor alone. But such concern is unlikely to occur because of what was accomplished when the pastor saw both spouses together in the first session. By insisting on seeing both spouses together the first time, Pastor Cowan demonstrated her commitment to fairness and her intention to take seriously the feelings and views of both spouses. Furthermore, in that first session Ron and Mary saw and experienced firsthand Pastor Cowan's intention not to take sides and to listen carefully to each of them.

Also, in the first session essential ground rules were presented and agreed to, a plan which included the explicitly stated possibility that one spouse might be seen once and the other perhaps two times. Finally, and perhaps of greatest importance, both spouses will be presented with the option to be seen twice individually by the pastor. If a spouse is seen only once it will be because that spouse has declined the opportunity to come in again to talk with the pastor. In fact, most persons will not take the opportunity for a second individual session, being satisfied with a single session. So if one spouse does elect to see the pastor for a second session, the other spouse rarely finds any cause for concern since that person saw little or no need to take advantage of a second meeting with the pastor.

To ensure productive meetings with each spouse, Pastor Cowan has important work to do before and after each counseling session. She will need to give careful attention to four important steps in the process (see the summary of this process on page 80). The first step is the reading and analysis of the responses to the Pastoral Marriage Counseling Questionnaire (PMCQ), which could each take a half hour to an hour. The next step is the preparation of a counseling outline that is structured around six essential questions. The third step is to be certain that the counseling room is suitably arranged. And after meeting with each spouse, the final step is one of sorting through and reflecting on all the information the pastor gathered from the individual counseling session.

Analyzing the Questionnaires

Besides the important information-gathering function of the PMCQ, the act itself of responding to all of the questions on the PMCQ can greatly help a husband and wife to look much more thoroughly at the possible sources and the dynamics of the discontent in their relationship. The PMCQ is not a simple assignment easily completed in ten or fifteen minutes, but the benefits to the spouses and to the counseling pastor far outweigh the time and effort required for a careful and thoughtful completion of the PMCQ.

The PMCQ presented in appendix B should be regarded as a model that can be revised or altered to suit each pastor's needs. The questionnaire as it appears now has been revised and updated to obtain information from couples essential for most marriage counseling circumstances.

Pastors will note that the questions on the PMCQ are wide ranging in their scope, addressing the present and the past in both the marriage and the spouses' personal lives. No matter how simple a presenting marriage problem may appear (e.g., a recently surfaced conflict over who will take out the garbage and the recycling), experienced counselors know that any problem may have deep roots that go far back in the relationship, even before the wedding, and/or far back in one or both spouses' lives. That is why the questions on the PMCQ are designed to illuminate as fully as possible all of the concerns troubling a couple.

Pastors will do best when they read the completed PMCQ with an eye for understanding instead of an eye for a quick solution or explanation to parishioners' marriage problems. Moreover, pastors can be reassured to know that most counselors will read and interpret each completed PMCQ differently. Pastors can take a relaxed approach about what parishioners write, and not try to arrive at elaborate or sophisticated interpretations of the data. In fact, the pastor's own questioning response, ("I don't understand this. I need more information about this area.") is a very good indicator of an area for further exploration with the counselee. Consultation with another professional person regarding the questionnaires, as long as a counselee's confidentiality is ensured, may also be a helpful option for the pastor.

When Pastor Cowan reads each questionnaire, she will not use a pen or pencil to make any checkmarks, circle any items, or otherwise make any marks on the questionnaires. She told the Nelsons that she would return their questionnaires to each of them, and Pastor Cowan knows that any marks she might put on the questionnaires may raise unnecessary concerns for Ron or Mary when they look over their returned questionnaires. They may be left to imagine and wonder what kind of significance Pastor Cowan read into any items that were marked, possibly unnecessarily raising their anxiety and concern. Instead, Pastor Cowan will keep a notepad handy as she reads each questionnaire, and will make her own notations on the notepad about areas and responses she thinks worthy of exploration with Ron and Mary.

The Exploratory Interview

Pastor Cowan will be the most helpful for Ron and Mary if she conducts a primarily exploratory interview. That is, her intention will be to ask Ron and Mary to offer more information about topics that seem especially relevant to the dynamics of the marriage. Therefore, as Pastor Cowan reads each questionnaire, she will be looking for written responses that suggest areas of interest or concern that may especially influence or contribute to how Ron and Mary relate to each other. The exploratory approach to those responses identified by Pastor Cowan will elicit the most information for the pastor's understanding. But more than that, an exploratory approach will help Ron and Mary to engage in an uncovering and searching process that may open up areas and dynamics they had not considered before. Such an exploratory approach to the individual counseling sessions is in sharp contrast to efforts by a pastor to inform, instruct, or otherwise attempt to impart knowledge or insight to the counselee.

The exploratory approach is illustrated when Pastor Cowan asks Mary about her responses to question number 8, about the use of the computer, and number 10, where Mary indicated that lack of communication is a factor in her marriage.

Pastor: Mary, I saw on your questionnaire that both you and Ron each spend about three hours every evening on the computer, answering e-mail, responding to chat rooms, and playing computer games. Can you say more about how the time you are both on the computer may have an impact on your marriage?

Mary: Well, it has bothered me for quite a while that we spend so much time on the computer at night. It's just so easy to get wrapped up in the computer instead of relating to each other.

Pastor: Yes, I also saw that you circled "lack of communication" as a problem area. Are you suggesting that there is a connection between your communication issues and the time each of you is spending on the computer?

Mary: Well, I hadn't thought about it much until I was answering those questions on the questionnaire the other night. Then I started adding up all the hours we sit staring at that screen, and—wow!—that's sure a lot of time Ron and I aren't talking to each other.

By responding to Pastor Cowan's requests for more information, Mary realized that she could not avoid any longer the fact that she and Ron have let their computers steal vital time from their marriage. Pastor Cowan did not inform or instruct Mary from the pastor's insight, such as, "Mary, I can see that you and Ron spend a lot of time on the computers while you say that you have communication problems. Obviously, you and Ron are letting your computers spoil your marriage!" Pastor Cowan might think she is very insightful and astute to share so much wisdom with Mary, but such a counseling response rarely if ever is helpful to a counselee and can even reinforce the counselee's resistance to change. Instead, Pastor Cowan made a quick note on the notepad in her lap about Mary's spirited reaction to her realization about what the computers were doing to the marriage. This, Pastor Cowan knew, could be an important issue to raise again when she asks later in the session, "What changes are you willing to make in yourself and in your own behavior for the improvement of your marriage?"

The exploratory interview can be very helpful for the counselee when it is used as Pastor Cowan used it to help Mary better understand an important aspect of her marriage. Therefore, pastors will want to read the

PMCQ with the intent of identifying the most promising areas for exploring with the counselee.

The PMCQ: Courtship and Marriage

1. *How did you and your spouse first meet?* It can be very helpful for many couples to review for the pastor how they first met and the hopes they had as their courtship began to develop. For many, one of their current goals in counseling will be to recover their original hopes and dreams for their marriage. In his book *Reclaiming the Dream: Marriage Counseling in the Parish Context*, Brian Grant vividly describes the dating process as "mutual inspections through a romantic haze."[1] Courting is the time when the couple develops a contract for meeting each other's hopes, needs, and dreams. But Grant observes that when the initial expectations for the marriage are not met and tensions rise, the couple will then "lose confidence in their ability to achieve the dream the marriage was supposed to be."[2] The pastor will better understand those original hopes and dreams by exploring this and the next question.

2. *What were your reasons for marrying your spouse?* Seriously conflicted marriages often reflect early decisions that got the marriage off to an uncertain start from the outset. In some difficult situations, spouses acknowledge that they really did not then, nor do they now, want to be married to their partner. Very hard decisions for both spouses usually have to be made following such a revelation. On the other hand, some couples have been able to salvage an ill-conceived relationship and, through much hard work leading to mutual commitment, have built an enduring marriage despite the questionable motives they had when they first decided to marry.

3. *What was your honeymoon like, and what were your feelings about it?* Responses to this question can offer important clues about the beginning of a marriage. A couple in agreement that the honeymoon was essentially a mutually positive experience may find it helpful in their current stage of conflict to recall the original positive beginnings of their marriage. In the case of an unsatisfying or troubled honeymoon, exploration of those first days and weeks of the marriage may offer important insights into the present tensions and problems facing the couple.

4. *Do you have any children? If yes, what are their names, ages, and grades in school?* If a couple does not have children, it may be informative for the pastor to inquire how that decision was made, using just those words, "How was that decision made?" and not just "Why?" It may, in fact, have not been

a decision but rather the result of unsuccessful and disappointing attempts to become pregnant. Or one partner may have made the decision, with the other spouse reluctantly concurring while inwardly longing someday to be a parent. Did the childless couple consider adoption, and how was that decision made? The answers to these questions may offer important insights into the communication pattern between husband and wife.

A pastor needs to remember that the arrival of each child brings new, stressful demands to the marriage. A pastor will often gain important information about a marriage by asking, "What changes do you recall occurred in your marriage with the arrival of each of your children? How were you particularly affected by those changes?"

The number of children and the range of their ages will offer indications about the kinds of parenting tasks the couple faces. Parents with two children under eighteen months of age have a different set of problems from a couple with two children in college. And the parents of two or three adolescent children are often dealing with concerns that can severely test the most harmonious marriage. Finally, whatever the constellation of parenting issues may be for a couple, the counseling pastor will want to know what each spouse thinks of the couple's communication process when making decisions about the children.

5. *Where do children outside the home live?* After children leave home, they remain a matter of much concern and even stress for many couples. Do any of the children live within a fifty-mile radius of their parents' home? If they do, does that mean they often return home? How often do the parents see their children who live greater distances from home? Are family reunions or gatherings with children important? Older couples may find helpful support and encouragement when their children live nearby and there is frequent interaction. This will especially be the case in situations where good relationships exist between the parents and their children. It is important that the pastor, when assessing where the children live, note also the quality of the relationships between the parents and their children and the impact of those relationships upon the parents' marriage. Furthermore, the role of grandchildren can be a very important factor for older couples and their marriage.

6. *If any children are no longer living, when and how did they die?* The death of a child, no matter at what age—even a stillborn infant—is a profound trauma for parents to experience. Such a death may mark a turning point of major proportions in the marriage. Such a crisis has the potential for either drawing a couple closer together or causing recurring tensions and conflicts.

Suicide is the third leading cause of death for young people ages 15 to 24. Data also indicate that some 3 million youth ages 12 to 17 thought seriously about suicide or attempted suicide in 2000.[3] Couples may also lose a child through illness, an automobile or motorcycle accident, or even homicide. When such a loss has occurred, the pastor should inquire how the parents adjusted to it, because it will usually represent a critical transition that may contribute significantly to the current stress in the marriage.

7. *Have you or your spouse been married before? If so, when, how, and why did that/those marriage(s) end?* The pastor wants to learn whether an earlier marriage is possibly continuing to affect adversely the present one. In some instances, this is an especially pertinent question when one of the spouses entered the present marriage before resolving feelings about the ending of the former marriage. Is there still unresolved grief about the death of one's first wife or husband? Did one partner remarry too soon after a divorce or the death of a spouse? Careful questions from the pastor regarding a former marriage will help a counselee consider whether and to what extent an earlier marriage is still an influence affecting the present marriage. Likewise, what has a remarried spouse learned from an earlier marriage?

8. *Is the amount of your time, or your spouse's time, spent on the computer and the Internet—or subjects of particular interest on the computer/Internet— a matter of concern for either of you? If yes, please explain.* Sitting in front of a computer can become a convenient diversion for distracting spouses from relating to one another or doing the difficult work of discussing and resolving differences and disputes. Indeed, the computer and the Internet can claim many hours every week while the other spouse is left to feel abandoned or emotionally neglected. The computer particularly becomes a destructive influence when it is used for viewing pornography or serves as the vehicle for a spouse to develop one or more "cyber-liaisons" with another lonely stranger. Pastors will want to be alert to the possibly negative role computers may play in their counselees' marriages.[4]

9. *Is the amount of time either of you spends away from home a matter of concern for either of you?* A not uncommon cause of marital tension is when one spouse is away from home fifty or more hours per week, and the other spouse is at home managing most of the details of the house and doing all of the child care. The absent spouse may come to feel like a visitor or a guest in his or her own house, effectively left out of the daily decision making that has to take place regarding the routine and maintenance of the house and the care, feeding, and chauffeuring of children to soccer games and music lessons.

Pastors should also be aware of the time that volunteer work can take from a marriage and family life. In fact, some of the pastor's most faithful and dedicated workers and officers in the church may be experiencing marital tension as a result of or somehow related to so many hours spent at church and away from home.

10. *Do the current problems in your marriage include any of the following?* This section of the questionnaire helps pinpoint specific complaints and concerns about the marriage.

a. *Lack of communication.* In some manner, most all marital conflicts are made worse by troubled patterns of communication. The busy pace of modern life can make it too easy and convenient for couples to withdraw from each other instead of talking about the problem areas in their relationship. Furthermore, most couples do not have the skills to interrupt their angrily escalating interactions when one or both of them feel hurt by something the other has said or done.

b. *Sexual or physical abuse.* The husband will be the abuser in most instances, but not always. Many victims of physical or sexual abuse often find it difficult to report or discuss the abusive behavior of a partner. The purpose of this question is to make it possible for the topic to be discussed in the counseling process.

There is never any justification for either partner, wife or husband, to be sexually or physically abused. Furthermore, a pastor should never forget that it can be very shaming for one or both partners to acknowledge to their pastor that abuse is a factor in the problems they are trying to resolve. A more detailed discussion of how the pastor may deal with instances of abuse appears in chapter 5.

c. *Infidelity.* In most marriages, the most damaging violation of trust occurs when a spouse has an affair. An affair may never be found out by the other partner, and so remains a secret. If the affair does come to light, it will ordinarily create a marital crisis of enormous proportions; in some cases the offended spouse will seek a divorce. On the other hand, some couples are able to do the hard work necessary for a reconciliation and for sufficient trust to be restored for their marriage to continue.

Sometimes a spouse who has had an affair earlier in the marriage feels sufficient guilt to consider telling his or her partner about the secret liaison. It is usually highly questionable whether revealing the secret will help the current marital relationship. Of course, the guilty spouse will need to make up his or her own mind. A pastor can be a valuable resource in such a situation, assisting the person to consider in a careful manner all the pros and cons of disclosing the earlier extramarital involvement.

As pointed out on the CPMC, marriage counseling cannot be successful if one of the spouses is currently engaged in a romantic or sexual relationship outside the marriage. Some persons will try to approach marriage counseling as a way of testing which matters more to them—their marriage or the extramarital relationship. *Marriage counseling cannot be effective unless the marriage is the primary relationship for both partners and both are committed to growth in their marriage and to the counseling process.* Consequently, to proceed with marriage counseling when one of the spouses is currently having an affair is to invite frustration and disappointment when the counseling fails to produce resolution and renewed commitment within the marriage.

Also, pastors can no longer ignore the possibility that the spouse involved in an extramarital sexual liaison may unknowingly be a carrier of the AIDS virus. In every situation the circumstances will be different, but the pastor will need to consider both the spouse's and the pastor's ethical responsibilities for informing the unknowing partner about the possibility of exposure to AIDS.

d. *In-law overinvolvement.* When Scripture says that a man shall leave his father and mother in order to live solely with his wife (Gen. 2:24), the point is clear that a new set of boundaries has been drawn for the sake of the marriage and the resulting family. In-laws, often with verbal assertions of loving concern, can overstep a couple's boundaries in countless ways, and a husband or a wife may often feel guilty about confronting excessive claims on their marital and family time and energy. A pastor can assist by helping the couple to see more clearly the boundaries they need to observe and protect for the sake of the primacy of their own relationship.

e. *Finances.* Disagreements over the management of money is a major source of conflict for many couples, and resolving differences in this area is all the more difficult when caring patterns for effective communication have deteriorated. Financial stress exists for couples in every income and age bracket. Moreover, conflicts about how to spend money often reflect fundamental differences over values. Cheryl exclaimed about Don's purchase of a large boat. "He just bought that boat for show. I think it's dumb! We need to remodel the kitchen far more than we need such an outrageously expensive boat. But do you think he listens to me? Of course not!" A pastor can be of considerable help in exploring the basic values that underlie a couple's different spending patterns.

f. *Problems relating to children.* Many days being a parent is an enormous challenge, often complicated all the more because what seems to work with one child can have the opposite effect with another child. Moreover, both parents naturally bring different experiences and backgrounds from their families of origin as they try to make the best decisions about their children. Consequently, the primary challenge for the parents is to listen to each other and to negotiate policies for child-rearing that reflect the essential views and feelings of both partners. Most couples will agree that if they are communicating effectively with each other they can manage to handle the crises that are to be expected with each child. The pastor can be a significant help by assisting couples to strengthen their own bonding and mutual understanding so they can approach parenting as supportive partners.

g. *Work-related problems.* Probably most married persons spend more waking time five or six days a week at work and in transit to and from work than they do at home. Many of the frustrations at work will be felt somehow by one's spouse. Certainly a required relocation to another community for the sake of one's work will greatly affect one's partner. And heightened pressures at work can prompt some to withdraw from their spouse, either into silence or into so-called workaholism. Pastors can provide a very helpful service to parishioners by enabling them to communicate about and sort through all their sources of work-related stress and their impact on the marriage.

Pastors must remember too that the work of maintaining a home can be as demanding as any job outside the home. Also, clergy (clergymen in particular) should be sensitive to how most women who work outside the home still feel responsible at the same time for all the chores and responsibilities at home. As a result, most women working outside the home feel they have two full-time jobs: their nine-to-five job and their homemaker's job. The sensitive pastoral counselor will attend to how husbands and wives are negotiating and sharing household responsibilities when both work outside the home. Moreover, these issues are not changed if one spouse maintains an office within the home. In fact, other stressful issues can be added by the problem of maintaining boundaries around one's office time and space in the midst of the relentless pressures and demands of the home environment.

h. *Alcohol or chemical abuse.* Alcohol or chemical abuse is always disruptive in a marriage and in the family. Sharon Wegscheider-Cruse has described the five roles that are typically played by family members where there is alcohol or chemical abuse.[5] The counseling pastor is encouraged to become familiar with the family dynamics and roles that often occur in families in order to cope with alcohol or chemical abuse by a family member. Frequently, the spouse of the alcoholic takes the role of *enabler*. In that role, the spouse supports the abuse despite the pain and emotional turmoil that typically are felt by the person in the role. The enabler usually makes excuses for the abusing spouse's behavior, and in other subtle ways supports the abusing spouse's pattern of alcohol or chemical dependence.

A pastor has important judgments to make in those cases where chemical or alcohol abuse is present in the marriage. Should steps be taken to get the dependent person into treatment? Consultation with a chemical dependency treatment facility can help the spouse or family and the pastor decide whether to make plans for a possible intervention that will lead the abusing spouse into treatment.[6]

Another important question is whether it is worth the time and effort to continue the marriage counseling if the chemically dependent spouse goes untreated or continues to use alcohol or other chemicals. As that question is being evaluated, the pastor must also decide how direct to be with both spouses about the abuse and its effect on the marriage. *In most instances, a straightforward, honest approach with the couple is much more effective than failing to identify and name the alcohol or chemical abuse as a destructive factor in the marriage.* Though the spouse who is accused of abusing alcohol or other chemicals may deny that such abuse is occurring, the fact that the other spouse is troubled about the behavior makes the matter an important issue for the marriage counseling process. If the marriage counseling does continue despite one or both spouses abusing alcohol or other chemicals, there should be plenty of evidence by the final session for the pastor to make a strong case for referral to a treatment facility or program if there is to be any hope for improvement or growth in the marriage.

i. *Sexual problems.* Even in the best of marriages, the communication and satisfaction of sexual needs is always a complex and delicate interaction. The process becomes immensely complicated when each partner naturally assumes that sexual intimacy for one's spouse is experienced in the same way as for one's own sexuality. This erroneous assumption often leads to much marital misunderstanding, frustration, and hurt.

In many instances, complaints about sexual problems may be symptomatic of a more basic intimacy problem for the couple. The primary role of intimacy for a husband and wife is emphasized in the book *Masters and Johnson on Sex and Human Loving*. Far from offering only a discussion of the biology and the mechanics of human sexuality, the book also focuses on the fundamental role of intimacy in a chapter entitled "Intimacy and Communication Skills." As the authors point out, "Intimacy can be defined as a process in which two caring people share as freely as possible in the exchange of feelings, thoughts, and actions. . . . Intimacy is generally marked by a mutual sense of acceptance, commitment, tenderness, and trust."[7]

Effective pastoral marriage counseling will help to facilitate the growth of renewed levels of intimacy. Pastors will help many couples improve their sexual relationship without ever discussing sex, the improvement coming as the counseling focuses on new ways for changing conflicted intimacy and communication patterns. Chapter 5 offers further discussion on the types of sexual problems that couples may report.

j. *Unfulfilled emotional needs.* People may experience a troubling emotional deficit in the marriage in one or more of three significant areas. One of those areas is the extent to which both spouses feel that their marriage is the *primary commitment* in each other's life. The emotional expectation for most persons is that they will be more important to their partner than any other person, object, or relationship. For example, many couples will especially feel the challenge today not to let either spouse's work demands and pressures outside the home assume an intrusive and competitive role that threatens the primacy of the marriage. Moreover, it is essential for a satisfying and fulfilling marriage that the primary importance of one's spouse be repeatedly and continually communicated in ways the other readily hears and understands. There are very few husbands and wives who do not have the basic emotional need to feel that they are first in their partner's affections and commitments.

The second essential emotional need for married persons is *trust*, which encompasses several dimensions of the relationship. Both partners need to know they can trust the other person in relationship with other people. Also, when both spouses are in each other's presence, they need to know that they can trust the other, that they will be safe both physically and psychically. Such trust permits spouses to be emotionally and intimately vulnerable to each other without fearing that they will be "beat up" or "beat on," either physically, sexually, or verbally.

The third main area of emotional need in secure marriages is best identified as *companionship*. Companionship in marriage includes facing together the innumerable difficult challenges of marriage and parenting, as well as going for a walk together on a Sunday evening or enjoying a quiet dinner in a special restaurant. Companionship is important because it fulfills the emotional need all married persons have for knowing that their partner wants to be with them and enjoys spending time with them. When companionship is missing, a marriage will fail to satisfy basic emotional needs in both spouses.

k. *Lack of spiritual growth.* Just as each individual's spiritual journey takes unique paths and directions, so couples will find many different ways for supporting each other toward growth in their faith. Some couples may report that they do not often talk about their faith but feel a spiritual closeness that is reassuring. Other couples may prefer a regular devotional pattern that includes reading Scripture and praying together. The sensitive pastor will encourage each couple to follow patterns that are comfortable and growth enhancing, and not discouraging or guilt producing. If a pastor can affirm whatever practices a couple reports are spiritually enlivening for them, they will feel supported for their spiritual intimacy and growth together.

l. *Premenstrual syndrome (PMS).* Either the wife or the husband may indicate that premenstrual syndrome is disruptive in the marriage relationship. In the popular culture, PMS is used imprecisely to attribute to the wife's monthly menstrual cycle the cause for nearly any conflict or tension in a marriage. The *Diagnostic and Statistical Manual of Mental Disorders* (DSM-IV) reports that it is estimated at least 75 percent of women acknowledge minor or isolated premenstrual changes. PMS may occur in 20 percent to 50 percent of women, and perhaps 3 percent to 5 percent of women experience severe symptoms that can be very distressing to a marriage. Symptoms vary from woman to woman, but three most common complaints include irritability, backaches or muscle pain, and bloating. The physical, psychological, and emotional symptoms of PMS typically occur during the one to two weeks before a menstrual period, and disappear soon after the onset of menstrual bleeding. When either spouse reports PMS as a disturbing factor in the marriage, the pastor should refer the woman to her physician for an accurate evaluation of her symptoms and the best treatment.[8]

11–13. *Who is going to make changes?* Nearly every spouse who comes to marriage counseling has no trouble naming the changes the other spouse needs to make for the marriage to improve. But trying to identify the changes one should make about oneself is much harder for most married persons to do. In fact, some would steadfastly maintain that they don't need to make any changes at all; they have no doubt that it is their spouse who is the source of all the problems in the marriage. So perhaps the most important question the pastor can ask each spouse is, "What are *you* willing to change?"

That question is intended to apply to the two areas a person can change. The first is one's attitudes or frame of mind. We are responsible for our own attitudes—impatience, judgmentalism, demanding expectations, and entitlement. We can change those negative attitudes to such positive attitudes as gratitude, patience, kindness, and helpfulness. In fact, we are far more accurate to recognize love as not being so much about a feeling as it is foremost an attitude of care and concern that we can choose.

The other area one can change about oneself is behavior. Behavior can be made quite specific. Instead of committing to be more caring toward his wife, Ken said that he would start loading the dishwasher and cleaning the kitchen every night after supper, and once a week he would clean the toilet in the master bathroom.

There will be changes that neither spouse will consider making. But given the freedom to make their own choice, people will often go to surprising lengths in the changes they will willingly make, because they recognize that making such changes is in their own best interest. And the possibility of having a loving marriage with far less conflict can, for many people, be very motivating for making significant changes in one's attitudes and behaviors.

The PMCQ: Family of Origin

The experiences and relationships people have in their formative years are very influential in the development of adult patterns of behavior. As the pastor inquires about personal family history, important clues may emerge that will be of help to the counselees as well as to the pastor. For example, it can be quite illuminating to recall the relationship that one observed as a child *between* one's parents. Also, relationships *with* one's own parents, and particularly the parent of the opposite gender, can be a significant influence in one's own marriage.

Furthermore, the role people have played in their family of origin may shed light on their reactions to current marital crises. The person who was the oldest child, responsible for the other children and perhaps for quite a few household chores, may respond to marital problems by attempting to take charge and becoming controlling. A child who played the martyr, letting others dump responsibility on him or her, may follow a similarly passive role in the marriage, while feeling very angry inside about being in such a seemingly powerless position. *It is essential for the pastor to inquire whether there is any history of alcohol or chemical abuse, as well as sexual or physical abuse, in a person's present or original family.* Questions 21 and 22 on the PMCQ offer the opportunity to respond to these issues. In those instances where there has been alcohol or chemical abuse in a spouse's family of origin, the pastor should inquire what effect the counselee feels such abuse had on one's childhood, adolescence, and emerging personality characteristics.[9] A pastor might also ask counselees who report abuse if they see any similar dynamics in their current marriage in comparison to those dynamics experienced as a child and adolescent in their family of origin.

Pastors should always be sensitive to the fact that both past and present experiences of physical or sexual abuse may be very difficult for most people to discuss. It can be especially difficult for a parishioner to talk about disturbing sexual experiences with a pastor of the opposite sex. The pastor will respect the counselee's willingness or reluctance, and listen with care to whatever the counselee is prepared to reveal and explore. In cases where persistingly disturbing memories of abuse are reported, the pastor should make a referral for personal counseling.

The pastor will proceed with the *Personal Information*, questions 23–35, in the same manner as with the foregoing questions and responses. The primary goal for the pastor throughout the PMCQ should be one of *seeking understanding*, not determining blame for the couple's problems. The pastor's intention to gain increased understanding provides the most helpful counseling context for each spouse. As the pastor asks questions, the counselee is more likely to begin gaining greater personal self-understanding and further insight into her or his marital dynamics.

Outline for Individual Counseling Sessions and the Six Key Questions

Before seeing Ron and Mary separately, Pastor Cowan will especially make note of six key questions that will ensure that the counseling session has a productive focus.[10]

Questions for the individual counseling sessions

1. How are things at the moment between you and your spouse?
2. How was it for you working on the questionnaire?
3. Did anything in particular stand out for you as you worked on the questionnaire?
4. Is there anything that we should be sure to discuss in this session?
5. What changes are you willing to make in yourself and in your own behavior for the improvement of your marriage?
6. Do you think another individual session would be helpful?

Pastor Cowan could have committed these six questions to memory, but she chose to write them down on a piece of paper that she kept on her lap during the counseling session. She will ask the first four questions at the beginning of the session. The fifth question will best be asked perhaps two-thirds of the way through the session after there has been discussion of the questionnaire. The sixth question near the end of the counseling session offers each spouse the opportunity to say whether a second individual session should be considered.

The six questions provide an outline or structure for a counseling session that is easy for a pastor to follow. Of course, the pastor will have prepared notes identifying specific areas in the questionnaire that should be explored further with the counselee. The pastor may even organize these notes so there is a natural sequence or outline to the questions he or she intends to ask about the counselee's responses to the questionnaire. *The pastor will raise those issues from the questionnaire after the counselee has responded to the pastor's fourth question, "Is there anything that we should be sure to discuss in this session?"*

The purpose of the first four questions is to encourage the counselee to reveal particularly important information and issues. If the pastor takes over right away by raising issues and questions the pastor thinks are particularly important, the pastor may miss very important, or even the most important, information about the counselee and the marriage. Moreover, it is likely that the information volunteered by the counselee in the early part of the session will be related to issues the pastor had identified on the questionnaire for exploration. As the counselee refers to those issues, the pastor can appropriately ask for further clarification and explanation.

Finally, it is especially important for the pastor to remember that the purpose of this session is for individual spouses to explore themselves and their own issues. Recalling item 5 in the Covenant for Pastoral Marriage Counseling, the individual session is not to be used by the counselee for rehearsing all the shortcomings and faults of the absent spouse. Focusing on the other spouse is a convenient way to avoid responsibility for oneself. If necessary, the pastor should be prepared gently but firmly to bring the counselees back to themselves, to their own contributions to the marital tensions, and finally to what changes they will make for the improvement of their marriage.

1. *How are things at the moment between you and your spouse?* Although it is likely that the status of the marriage has not changed significantly, the pastor might learn that a significant change for the better or for the worse has occurred. And if a crisis, such as a fight or an argument, has just taken

place that is upsetting for the spouse, the pastor will very possibly decide to give some attention for a few minutes to that troubling concern. However, the primary focus for this counseling session—the counselee's responses to the questionnaire—should not be lost.

This initial question also has diagnostic value for the pastor. The counselee's response will offer some immediate, tentative data about the severity and depth of the marital conflict and tension. Likewise, it can be instructive for the pastor to make a mental comparison of each spouse's response to this question. If one spouse says the relationship is worsening and the other says things are improving, the pastor will want to explore what lies behind the incongruent perceptions. If both partners offer a similar assessment of the current status of their relationship, the pastor can assume that both spouses are likely offering an accurate evaluation.

2. *How was it for you working on the questionnaire?* The transition from the current status of the marriage to the questionnaire can easily be made with the pastor thanking the counselee for completing the questionnaire. The second question then follows naturally.

The purpose of this question is twofold. If the counselee had any kind of a negative response to the questionnaire, it is important for the counseling process that the negative feelings be aired at this point. If these feelings aren't discussed, they will likely surface somewhere else in the counseling process as perhaps a disturbing distraction. If the counselee verbalizes the negative feelings at this point, the counselee will most likely find it easier to move on and deal with the questionnaire.

The second reason for asking this question is that it may immediately lead the counselee and the pastor to valuable material for further exploration. Perhaps most often the counselee will say the questionnaire was "okay," meaning that it was a long but otherwise unremarkable exercise. However, it is not unusual for a counselee to remark that one or more questions touched on very significant, painful, or insight-generating areas of the marriage or the counselee's earlier life. These are the areas that the pastor will want to explore further with the counselee.

3. *Did anything in particular stand out for you as you worked on the questionnaire?* Obviously, this is a backup question to the previous question. It is entirely possible for a counselee to offer no particularly significant response to the second question, but then to name one or more important areas in response to this third question. Again, the pastor is using these questions in order to explore where the most relevant or troubling areas are in the counselee's marriage or the counselee's personal life as they may relate to the marriage. These are the areas the counselee needs

to understand better, especially as they influence the marital relationship. As the pastor asks questions for clarity the counselee will be aided toward further personal exploration and understanding.

4. *Is there anything that we should be sure to discuss in this session?* This question invites the counselee to raise any important issues that she or he feels are much more easily and more safely explored in this individual session where the other spouse is not present. Indeed, this question gives the counselee permission and encouragement to raise important concerns that the counselee might otherwise be reluctant to mention or that could be completely missed if the pastor dominates the session with the pastor's own questions and agenda. This question also opens the way for the counselee to raise relevant and personal concerns about the marriage that were not adequately addressed by the questionnaire. After affirming and clarifying the counselee's response to this question, the pastor will turn to issues that need to be explored on the PMCQ. The fifth question will come about two-thirds of the way through the session.

5. *What changes are you willing to make in yourself and in your own behavior for the improvement of your marriage?* Virtually all persons come to marriage counseling absolutely convinced that their spouse must make major changes if the marriage is to improve. They are sure that the sooner the counselor can get their spouse to change, the sooner the marriage problems will be resolved. Likewise, they are certain that their spouse's expectations for change by them are unreasonable.

This may be the most important question the pastor asks each spouse. Some persons will be shocked or dismayed when they consider, possibly for the first time, that their own behavior is contributing to the marital problems. Furthermore, the question also suggests the essential point that it is futile for a spouse to attempt to improve the marriage by trying to change his or her marriage partner. In so many words, the pastor tells individual spouses that they can only change themselves. Or, as some marriage therapists have aptly put it, paraphrasing President Kennedy's famous challenge, "Ask not what your partner can do for you; ask what you can do for your partner."[11]

The pastor will encourage each spouse to make personal changes that are not conditioned upon changes in the other partner. When spouses are willing to make positive changes regardless of their partner's changes, there is good reason to hope for significant and lasting change for the better in the marriage.

6. *Do you think another individual session would be helpful?* In her first meeting with Ron and Mary Nelson, Pastor Cowan said that she would

meet individually with each of them one or two times. Near the end of the individual session with each of them, Pastor Cowan asks this important question about the possibility of a second individual counseling session.

This question clearly inquires about the counselee's level of interest and motivation for a second individual session. Most likely the usefulness and productivity of a second individual counseling session will be commensurate with the counselee's level of interest in the session. Furthermore, if the counselee has little motivation for the second individual meeting, then the pastor will be left to take full charge of the second session and do most of the work. The counselee will very likely get nothing of much benefit from such a second session. However, if in the first individual session a counselee has begun to explore very significant or potentially illuminating and insightful issues, the person will often welcome a second individual session and the opportunity to look more closely at those issues. By putting this question to the counselee, the counselee is given the opportunity to take responsibility for her or his own counseling and for her or his own examination of self and the marriage.

Perhaps the pastor will feel that there are personal issues for the counselee that deserve closer examination. Or there may be areas and responses on the questionnaire that were not covered in the first individual session because of a lack of time. The pastor certainly can point out these areas that could, and perhaps should, be dealt with in a second session. The pastor should remember, however, that the less invested the counselee is in a second individual session the less productive and helpful that session is likely to be. More often than not, counselees will be satisfied with what occurs in the first individual counseling session and will not feel a need for a second individual session.

Inquiry about extramarital affairs. Some pastoral counselors make it a point during an individual session with a spouse to inquire specifically if the counselee is currently involved in an extramarital affair or ever has been during the course of the marriage. Likewise, the counselor may follow that question with a question as to whether the counselee has ever had reason to suspect his or her spouse of being involved in an affair.

Though the question about a possible extramarital liaison is not inappropriate, it can be an awkward and unnecessary question for a pastor to ask. Moreover, the issue was raised on the CPMC form by the statement that full commitment to the marriage is necessary for productive marriage counseling. And question 10 on the PMCQ provides an opportunity for counselees themselves to identify infidelity as an issue in the marriage, either their own or their spouse's. It seems reasonable to assume that in most instances when a spouse is involved in an affair the issue will some-how be reported by the husband or wife, often in the first session. Of course, some counselees are very good at keeping secrets, so there is always the possibility that an affair will never be disclosed.

Closing the counseling session. In the individual counseling sessions, as in the joint sessions, the pastor will decide the best way to use faith and Scripture resources as part of the counseling process. The use of Scrip-ture and prayer should emerge naturally from the interview to reflect the presence of God's love and to affirm the counselee's own best intentions and hopes, without ever becoming a manipulative exercise that denies the deeper conflicts in human emotions.

Arranging the Room

For the first counseling session Pastor Cowan made sure that the seating permitted each person to see the others equally well, with the chairs an equal distance from each other. This same seating arrangement will also work well for the individual counseling sessions. The pastor will be seated away from the desk so there can be a direct conversation with the counselee. The placing of the chairs should easily provide for indirect eye contact so the counselee does not feel stared at by the pastor. A small table between the chairs is typically not obtrusive. Once again, there should be a box of tissues at hand and a clock in plain sight for everyone to see.

Reflecting on the Data

In a spirit of prayerful deliberation, the pastor should consider all that has been learned in the individual sessions with each spouse. In most instances, a pastor will be impressed with the pain felt by both spouses, who in their own way are trying their best to cope. Yet most often the pas-tor will recognize defeating patterns engaged in by each spouse that seem only to aggravate and make the marital conflicts worse instead of leading to resolution. Likewise, the pastor will often see what appear to be simple or elementary changes that partners could make but that they steadfastly refuse to make for reasons they think make sense. Nonetheless, the coun-seling pastor will resist the temptation to take sides or place blame on one spouse or the other. Likewise, the pastor will also resist the equally com-pelling temptation to prepare a list of "answers" or "solutions" to present to the couple when they return together.

Relationship-Destructive Compulsive Behaviors

Problem gambling and sexual addiction can be very destructive to a marriage, though it is unlikely that both will be practiced by the same person. Furthermore, these are behaviors engaged in by a person despite continuing shame or remorse and painful consequences to themselves and others. If a pastor hears a suggestion from either spouse that one or the other is engaged in out-of-control sexual or gambling behavior, including on the Internet, the pastor should be careful to clarify the basis for the report and *not* to use either label of sexual addiction or compulsive gambling. There are helpful books and online resources that can be informative for the pastor. However, diagnosis should not be attempted by the pastor, regardless of what conclusions have been reached by one or both of the spouses. An appropriate diagnosis in these cases should be made by a physician, psychologist, or a professional specializing in the treatment of sexual addiction or compulsive gambling. If a pastor has reason to believe a couple is dealing with either of these problems, the pastor is urged first to discuss the facts of the case with a professional consultant to determine if a referral is in order. If a referral for treatment is made, the other spouse should also be referred to a support resource for family members. Progress in the marriage is very unlikely until the problem is effectively treated.[12]

Counselee Mental and Emotional Status

The pastor should also give consideration to how each spouse behaved and spoke in the individual session. A pastor can assess the impressions made by a counselee in four important areas.

Mood. What is the person's prevailing mood? What are the person's dominant feelings? During a marital crisis, it is not unusual for spouses to experience considerable anger, anxiety, or depression. Disturbance in normal appetite and sleep patterns can be important clues about how upset a person is over the marital tension. The pastor should also consider if there is any evidence of mood disturbance that is too pervasive to be wholly attributable to the marital crisis.

Judgment. An estimation should be made of each person's capacity for making appropriate decisions. How will this person respond in a crisis? Can this person make decisions that represent his or her own best interests?

Abstraction. Does the person think in highly abstract terms, or is the person more concrete about reaching decisions? For example, can the pastor talk with the husband about an egalitarian marriage in which role reversal from the traditional marriage is welcomed and valued? Or does the pastor have to speak in very specific language about the husband washing the dishes while his wife takes the car to have the oil changed?

Reasoning and perception of reality. The pastor should note if there is any apparent irrational quality to a person's reasoning. Does the person's thinking follow a logical sequence that makes sense? Does either spouse reflect undue concern for what others may be thinking or saying about them? The pastor should take particular notice of any reports by a person that he or she has heard or seen objects or people that others would not have heard or seen if they had been present. The pastor should recommend psychiatric assessment if he or she observes or learns of any serious disturbance in a counselee's reasoning or perception of reality.

Faith Resources

Is the person's faith a positive source of help during the marital crisis, or are the person's religious beliefs a source of disappointment or frustration? It is not extraordinary for faithful Christians to experience considerable doubt during a major crisis such as the deterioration of a marriage. The best pastoral care is to permit the person to express negative thoughts while offering pastoral support to the dimensions of faith that hold out a legitimate hope for the person in crisis.

Conclusion

It is entirely appropriate for a pastor, following the individual counseling sessions with both spouses, to feel virtually overwhelmed with information and short on understanding. Indeed, a pastor should be suspicious about any firm conclusions that emerge, because such conclusions may not fully take account of all of the complexities in the marriage conflict. It is not the pastor's role when meeting again with the couple to attempt to give them an elaborate explanation for why they are having marital problems. The pastor may offer some tentative ideas, but any explanations that have the appearance of fixing the blame on one or the other spouse will jeopardize the counseling process. Rather, the pastor's sincere search for understanding will help the couple to take seriously their own search for understanding. The real question for the couple when they return together to see the pastor is not "What has the pastor figured out about our marriage?" but rather, "What is it that each of us has been learning in this counseling process, and what are the best decisions each of us is willing to make now?"

Pastor Cowan has taken a significant step toward helping a troubled couple by talking separately with the spouses and exploring with each of them important issues at the heart of their marriage. Though much may still be unclear about what the outcome of the counseling will be and what decisions the Nelsons may each make, it is clear that the couple is engaged in a counseling process that offers promise for each of them and their marriage. Now that the spouses have a better understanding of their relationship, there certainly is the possibility that the counseling process of encounter and dialogue will open encouraging options that earlier had not been envisioned. So with a realistic hope plus concerned caring for both spouses, Pastor Cowan continues with the counseling plan and arranges now to meet again with the couple.

The Four-Step Process for Meeting with Each Spouse

1. Read and analyze responses to the Pastoral Marriage Counseling Questionnaire.
2. Prepare a counseling outline around six essential questions:
   a. How are things at the moment between you and your spouse?
   b. How was it for you working on the questionnaire?
   c. Did anything in particular stand out for you as you worked on the questionnaire?
   d. Is there anything that we should be sure to discuss in this session?
   e. What changes are you willing to make in yourself and in your own behavior for the improvement of your marriage?
   f. Do you think another individual session would be helpful?
3. Arrange the counseling room.
4. Sort through and reflect on the information gathered in the individual session.

Chapter Four

The Plan for the Final Two Sessions

The good-enough relationship is not problem-free. . . . But they preserve the relationship because they *choose* to be in it, because they are able to rediscover what makes it *worth it* for them, because its gratifications outweigh its trials. . . . They know that, in the river of time, it is with this person and on this raft that they choose to travel.

—Mark A. Karpel, *Evaluating Couples: A Handbook for Practitioners*

This chapter covers:

~ Reasons for discontinuing marriage counseling

~ Proceeding with the marriage counseling

~ Encouraging each spouse to make changes

~ The "growth task" before the final session

~ Options for when counseling appears not to go well

~ The pastor's preparation for the final counseling session

~ Criteria for three recommendation options

~ The process in the final counseling session

~ Continuing pastoral care

Pastor Cowan eagerly greets the Nelsons as she welcomes them outside her church office. "Hi, Ron! Hi, Mary!" Motioning toward her office, she invites them in. Three chairs are arranged as in the first counseling session, with tissues and a clock nearby. Pastor Cowan asks Mary and Ron to be seated as she picks up her notes and tablet and takes her own seat.

Without trusting her visual observations of smiles and body language, Pastor Cowan wants to hear directly from Ron and Mary if there is any immediate tension between them. It is not extraordinary for a couple to have a fight or heated disagreement in the car on the way to the pastor's office, cover the tension with broad smiles that can defy any counselor's closest scrutiny, then, after deceiving the counselor and wasting time for an hour, get back in the car and on the way home pick up the fight right where it left off an hour earlier. So Pastor Cowan begins by saying to the Nelsons, "I would like each of you to give me a weather report on the mood between the two of you at this moment. You know: stormy, sunny, cloudy, or whatever it is for each of you." Though a little surprised by the request, the Nelsons immediately recognize what their pastor wants to know. Pausing for a moment, Ron looks at Mary and smiles cautiously, then says, "I'd say that there are some broken clouds with bits of sunshine peeking through." Then Pastor Cowan turns to Mary. "What's your weather report, Mary?" Mary looks back at Ron with a trace of a smile, and then replies to her pastor, "Well, to tell the truth, a thunderstorm blew through about two hours ago, but there does appear to be some sunshine on the horizon."

If, however, the Nelsons report that they are in the midst of a big storm right now that started ten minutes before coming to the counseling session, Pastor Cowan might see no other choice but to discuss the issues causing the argument. Attempting to discuss anything else will be pointless as long as the Nelsons are so painfully preoccupied with their argument. But in this particular situation the storm has already passed, hints of sunshine are visible through the clouds, and Pastor Cowan can expect the Nelsons to be able to give their full attention to broader questions about their marriage. Pastor Cowan had decided earlier that there was no reason to discontinue the marriage counseling process following the individual counseling sessions.

Reasons for Possibly Discontinuing the Marriage Counseling

There are four common issues that should cause the pastor to consider whether to make an immediate referral for other professional help. If a referral is to be made after the individual counseling sessions, the best practice is to make the referral when the pastor is meeting with both spouses together so they both hear together their pastor's recommendation and explanation for the referral. The four most likely marital crises that can make continued pastoral counseling questionable include a current extramarital affair, alcohol or chemical addiction or abuse, physical or sexual abuse, and emotional or mental distress at such a disturbing level that immediate medical assessment is required for medication and/or psychotherapy. Furthermore, when any one of these issues must be discussed with a couple, and decisions are made about the pastor's possible continuing role as a counselor, a primary rule should be observed that *the pastor cannot function as both a counselor for the marriage and an ongoing counselor to one of the spouses.* If for whatever reason the decision is made for the pastor to continue as the counselor for one of the spouses on an individual basis, then the partners should be seen by another professional for their marital relationship. Likewise, the pastor also should not attempt to continue as the counselor to both spouses individually at the same time. There is an inherent conflict of interest that makes it inadvisable for any counselor to engage in extended individual counseling at the same time with both spouses.

Extramarital Affairs

While there are always exceptions to every rule, these three guidelines should be considered by pastors when deciding how to handle the disclosure in the individual sessions of current romantic or sexual liaisons outside the marriage.

1. Marriage counseling has no possibility for being successful unless both spouses are committed to the marriage without other competing relationships. This guideline excludes the possibility of a spouse participating in marriage counseling in order to explore whether to remain with the affair partner or the marriage partner.

2. If the person involved in the affair is not prepared to end that relationship, the pastor should recommend that the marriage counseling be discontinued, no matter how awkward that recommendation may be. Likewise, pastors have very good reason to be suspicious if a spouse attempts to reassure the pastor that a current affair will be terminated. Typically, the ending phase of most affairs takes weeks if not many months as one or both parties to the affair usually find excuses and means for continuing contact with each other. Marriage counseling will not be productive while one of the spouses is going through the emotional distraction and turmoil of such an ending phase to an affair.

In the second joint counseling session, the explanation offered by the pastor to the other spouse is that because of new information that has come to light in the individual session the pastor is recommending personal counseling for the first spouse. So if Mary, during an individual session, had revealed that she is involved currently with another man, Pastor Cowan should say to Ron and Mary that personal counseling for Mary is recommended, with the marriage counseling being discontinued until Mary has resolved some personal issues. At this point Mary may decide to disclose the affair, or Ron may "put two and two together" and confront Mary with the possibility that she is having an affair. Such a situation can be expected to be very distressing for both spouses, requiring sensitive and wise pastoral responses.

3. The pastor should also consider recommending supportive counseling for the other spouse. Though the second spouse may or may not suspect that an affair is a factor in the marriage, individual supportive counseling can help that spouse cope with the considerable stress and uncertainty of having the marriage counseling discontinued.

Alcohol or Chemical Abuse

As most pastors know, the presence of alcohol or chemical abuse in a marriage creates a difficult situation for the counselor to evaluate.[1] If, in fact, both spouses have, with some degree of willingness, come to the pastor for help, the pastor may regard that as a major achievement in and of itself. Nonetheless, the pastoral counselor has two important options to consider.

1. Evidence from the individual counseling sessions may show that the abuse is of such proportions that an addictive pattern is suspected. A significant test is if the marital conflicts and tension typically escalate whenever one or both spouses use alcohol or other chemicals.

Until the addictive behavior or the abusive use of alcohol or chemicals is treated or effectively discontinued, marriage counseling cannot be expected to be very useful. The pastor needs to consider reporting this conclusion to both spouses, with the option that the addicted or abusing spouse go to a treatment center or agency for evaluation and the other spouse become involved with Al-Anon. The pastor can indicate that once those steps have been taken and the first spouse is no longer using alcohol or other chemicals, counseling will be much more promising and the pastor will then be very glad to meet with the couple to evaluate their marriage.

2. The pastor may determine that alcohol or chemical use is a factor in the marital conflicts but that it does not appear an addictive pattern is present. Either spouse may acknowledge that on some occasions the use of alcohol has been excessive, with a resulting negative impact on the marriage. So the pastor must make a judgment, a decision that should be shared openly with both spouses when the joint counseling sessions are resumed. The pastor must also have obtained the permission of each spouse in order to report information from the individual sessions.

> Pastor: Beverly, in your individual session last week you talked about the times over the past two years when you know that you have had too much to drink at office parties. Then you have come home, and you and Earl have invariably gotten into an argument. This pattern has happened three times in the past two years, the last time being about two months ago. Earl, you reported that you and Beverly have talked about choosing some new friends who do not need to mix so much alcohol with their socializing. Neither one of you feels that the other has a pattern of regularly abusing alcohol. We can continue this marriage counseling process on that assumption. I believe the test is whether in fact you can make genuine progress on your marriage, and whether the alcohol completely stops being a factor in any marital conflicts.

Physical or Sexual Abuse

Continued marriage counseling will not be productive if either spouse feels abusively intimidated by the other. Threatening behavior is not limited to physical contact, but includes such violent expressions as throwing things, shouting, and slamming doors.[2] The rebuilding of a marriage requires a relationship in which trust can be nurtured and there is encouragement for taking risks and being vulnerable in sharing feelings with one another. Renewed and increased openness to one another will not take place if either spouse is living under the threat of physical or sexual retaliation.

Therefore, if either spouse reports physical or sexual abuse, when the spouses return together after their individual sessions the pastor should talk frankly with them about ending the marriage counseling and making a referral. The pastor needs to say to both of them that the fear of physical or sexual abuse will prevent progress through the counseling toward rebuilding trust and intimacy. Furthermore, the pastor can explain that a specialist in domestic violence treatment and counseling should be the one to assist the victim and the couple to evaluate the likelihood of the abuse reoccurring and representing a continuing threat to the marriage.

The couple should be referred to a domestic abuse treatment program for evaluation of the abusing spouse. The victim should be advised of all available resources, including a domestic violence hotline, contact information about shelters, and legal and police protection if necessary. The victim should also receive further counseling assistance, either through a domestic abuse treatment program or through individual counseling, as decisions are made about the best choices for the victim, the children and family, and the marriage. A more complete discussion of pastoral options follows in chapter 5.

Referral for Personal Counseling

In the course of the individual sessions, it may become evident to the pastor that the emotional concerns and stresses of one of the spouses must be given as much attention as the marriage problems. Of course, it may be difficult to distinguish whether a spouse's severe anxiety or depression is because of the marital tensions, or whether it is a factor contributing to those conflicts.

The pastor's decision is whether to offer a referral immediately at the second joint counseling session, or to proceed through to the third and final joint session. A severe and pressing or life-threatening crisis will warrant an immediate referral for individual attention for a medical or psychological evaluation. In other cases, continuing the marriage counseling model through to the third and final joint session will provide opportunity for pastoral support while helping the couple to make sound decisions for the next steps that they take.

When referring a spouse for immediate professional attention, it is essential that the pastor do so in such a manner as to minimize any appearance or suggestion that the marriage problems are all attributable to the spouse being referred. Such a conclusion may all too readily be reached by the other spouse, offering a convenient excuse for not recognizing or acknowledging his or her own contribution to the problems in the marriage.

Proceeding with the Marriage Counseling

Pastor Cowan has decided there are no reasons for recommending to Ron and Mary that the marriage counseling be discontinued with a referral. So Pastor Cowan next asks both spouses to disclose any new ideas or feelings they have about their marriage and how they might best resolve their conflicts. This is an important question for both spouses to answer.

> Pastor: I appreciate the effort both of you invested in responding to the questionnaire and the concerns you discussed with me when I saw each of you separately. I am wondering now what things you have learned or feelings you have had, either from the counseling process so far, or from any conversations you have had with each other, or just from your own personal thoughts.

It is essential to note that Pastor Cowan does not begin the session with any comments or analysis about what she thinks is the problem or source of the marital conflict. This is not the time for Pastor Cowan to render an "expert opinion" based on all the written material and the individual sessions with both partners. Almost certainly, any analysis that the pastor might offer at this point, even if it were requested by the husband and wife, will very likely be discounted or disregarded by one or both of them. Besides, what is really important at this point is what the husband and wife think the problems are, along with any new ideas they have for resolving those problems together. Ron and Mary might respond to Pastor Cowan's inquiry in this manner:

> Ron: I think that I am seeing a little more clearly why we so often get into painful and heated arguments about the demands my career puts on me to relocate and move the family every three or four years. I believe that the security of our family is directly related to my job security and the substantial raises I get every time I take a new position elsewhere in the company. In fact, my willingness to relocate has helped me to move up a lot faster than a lot of other guys. Management knows very well who I am, and they like me. And I've always assumed that because Mary's family moved around the country a lot for her dad's career when she was growing up that Mary would naturally understand and even enjoy the chance to look at new

scenery in a new city in another three years. Now I see that I was making a wrong assumption. I guess I'm not Mary's father. I'm also realizing that some other things are more important to Mary than being married to a highly paid "rising star." I really want to work with Mary to make the necessary changes so we can have a better marriage and real emotional stability for our children.

Pastor: Those sound like very important insights, Ron. Have you shared these thoughts yet with Mary?

Ron: No, there hasn't been a chance because we've been so busy taking the kids to soccer practices and trumpet lessons and Scout meetings. But, Mary, I'm seeing now that emotional security in our family is even more important than just getting another big raise by moving halfway across the country.

Pastor: What's your reaction, Mary, to what Ron is saying? Would you look at him and tell him directly?

Mary: I can hardly believe, Ron, what I'm hearing you say! I've been trying for so long to tell you that I hated it when I was growing up, and I lived in dread when Dad would come through the door and announce that we were going to move again. And Mom just smiled and stuffed her feelings and started packing the boxes. And I had to start making new friends all over again in some new place I'd never heard of before. That's why I react so emotionally and irrationally when you think you are bringing good news home about taking a new position somewhere out of state for more money. Security for me is knowing that I won't have to face another move and that we and our children can make friends we won't have to say good-bye to. We have enough money. I want you and me now to build a marriage together right here, for a long time in this town, that is based on emotional security and stability for us and for our children.

This counseling session is off to a good start because (1) it builds on the spouses' own insights, (2) both spouses agree about the source of some of their significant conflict and are willing to work together on the problem, (3) they talk about and describe themselves instead of characterizing, blaming, or attacking the other person, and (4) they are talking directly to each other instead of going through the pastor. These positive behaviors by Ron and Mary are essential for resolving marital conflict, and should be encouraged by the pastor at every opportunity in the counseling process.

Unfortunately, many marriage counseling sessions typically do not consist of such respectful and productive communication between the husband and wife. Destructive and negative exchanges are readily recognized by the pastor when one spouse analyzes the other, makes unfavorable generalizations about the other, and uses the word "you" in an accusatory manner while failing to disclose any information about herself or himself. When such attacking or blaming occurs, the best intervention by the pastor will be to interrupt the cycle by (1) focusing on the blamer's feelings while drawing attention away from the spouse who is being blamed and (2) clarifying the blamer's issue(s). It is essential that the blamer feel that he or she has been heard and taken seriously, without the other spouse feeling attacked.

One need not agree with the blamer in order to acknowledge the blamer's troubled feelings and the blamer's issues. Usually, once a blamer feels heard the blamer will calm down and stop accusing the other spouse. For example, Ron could have made the following blaming response instead of the personally insightful reply above.

> Ron: Well, I've gotten a lot out of the questionnaire and the individual session, Pastor. I see plainly now that the fact of the matter is that Mary has never understood how hard I work just so she and the kids can have a little security. She fails to see that nothing has changed from when her own father had to work so hard, even though it meant moving every couple years. Frankly, I think if Mary grew up and got over being so shy and thinking everyone is looking at her she'd make a lot of friends no matter where we might live or how long or how short a time we live there! If you're friendly, Mary, you can make friends fast.

> Mary: Ron, I know all about being friendly. You don't have to tell me how to be friendly. I've had to learn how to make friends fast just to survive, because you think a big salary in this family can buy love and give your children everything they need!

> Ron: You see, Pastor, what thanks I get for making it possible for Mary to be free to have time for church and the six other clubs

she belongs to. She has a good life, but hasn't figured out it takes money to make that all possible.

Pastor: Ron, I want to interrupt you to make sure I understand your concerns. You have taken very seriously that it's your job to bring home the money your family needs in order to live comfortably. You've always been a hard worker, and you can't help it that to make a top salary requires that you and your family move every three or four years. But, perhaps worst of all, you feel unappreciated by Mary for all your hard work and dedication. Is that close to what you are saying?

Ron: Yes, that's it, Pastor. I mean, I get the impression that Mary thinks my intention is to make her miserable when what I'm trying to do is to give our family the best life possible.

Pastor: And it really bothers you that Mary doesn't seem to see what your real intentions are for her and your family.

Ron: That's absolutely right. And I don't know how to get that through to Mary. So I have to admit, that's when I start blaming her when I feel so frustrated.

Pastor: So when you are frustrated that's when you blame Mary. But blaming Mary doesn't work very well, does it? If you could find better ways to talk with Mary, maybe you could talk about your frustration without blaming her for what you feel.

Ron: I know Mary stops listening when I blame her for everything. If I stop blaming Mary, maybe she'll hear me better, and then I might not feel so frustrated. I don't know about Mary, but that would sure make my life easier!

At this point, Pastor Cowan has the option of engaging in further exploring and clarifying with Ron, or of turning to Mary and asking for her views. The pastor's careful attention, while conversing directly with each spouse, to focusing on feelings and clarifying basic issues helps each spouse to learn, from a less threatening vantage point as an observer, important new information about the other's feelings and attitudes.

Pastoral counselors will also note that Pastor Cowan did not turn to Mary and ask, "How does it make you feel when Ron says you need to grow up and get over being so shy?" This kind of unfortunate approach to couple counseling can be very destructive, and this is compounded by the equally erroneous assumption that we are made to feel certain ways because of our partner's behavior. The effective pastoral counselor will never ask the question, "How does that make you feel when . . . ?"

Making Changes

An important step in this second joint session is for the pastor to explore with both partners what changes they think they are willing to make for the improvement of their marriage.

> Pastor: When you came for marriage counseling it was probably quite clear to you what changes the other should make so you could have fewer problems in your marriage. However, I want to ask each of you now what changes you yourself are prepared to make so there can be improvements in your relationship. At the same time, I understand that neither of you will make all the changes that the other wants, but what really matters is what each of you is willing to do so you both will feel better about your marriage.

> Mary: You are right, Pastor. I won't be changing my feelings against moving our family to a new city every three or four years. However, I know that I should be much more expressive to Ron about how grateful I am for how he works so hard to provide for our family. So, Ron, I will say thank you at least once a week, and even be sure to make one of your favorite desserts once a week! Also, if we start to see that our budget is getting too tight, I'm ready to start talking with you about how I might look for a part-time job outside the home, maybe fifteen to twenty hours a week. I think I could love working in a fabric store, and a few extra thousand dollars a year might really help us.

> Ron: I know that I need to change my attitude about being a corporate climber. It scares me, because in this company if you aren't moving up you may get moved out. But we can find some way to survive if we stay here and don't move. It won't be easy for me, but I will no longer bring up the issue of moving. However, I'm not ready to cut back my hours at work to become a "house husband" doing the cooking and the laundry. Maybe we'll have to hire someone to come in and clean

the house if you go to work part-time. I like my work at the office, and I don't want my manager to ever think I'm not being as productive as I've always been.

Pastor Cowan can rightly feel that some significant progress has occurred with Mary and Ron making these commitments to change. If couples are reluctant to talk about changes they each will make, or if they add sarcastic or disparaging comments such as "It won't do any good," or "I've heard those promises before," the pastor's tentative assessment should be that resolution of the couple's conflicts will very likely require longer-term counseling. Such an assessment should not necessarily be discouraging; rather, it should help the pastor set realistic expectations for what can or cannot be accomplished by the couple within the limits of short-term counseling.

Taking Action

Under the best of circumstances, a troubled couple will be ready at this stage to commit themselves to engage in some homework together or, better, a "growth task" before the next—and final—joint counseling session. The pastor has used the second joint session to explore what changes each spouse is ready to make. Using their readiness to make some limited changes, the pastor now can help the couple commit themselves to some specific tasks. These will be new behaviors for each of them for the sake of making positive changes in their relationship.

The pastor should exercise some caution and be wise about the growth task to be undertaken by the couple. It is best if the partners decide for themselves what they will accomplish before the next counseling session. Anything given or imposed on a couple by the pastor has considerably less likelihood of being attempted or accomplished. If husband and wife can design their own growth task, and thus have a greater sense of ownership for the project, they are more likely to complete the project. Pastor Cowan puts the matter to Ron and Mary in this fashion:

> Pastor: Mary and Ron, you have both offered to make some impor-
> tant changes. I heard some things about favorite desserts, say-
> ing thank you, Mary taking a part-time job, and Ron no longer
> suggesting a move. I think I was hearing that you will work
> together to put down your roots in this community and to
> make it your home for your family. If that is the case, I'm won-

dering what specific, concrete, new steps you both would be willing to take in the next week or so before we meet again.

Ron: You know, Mary, that a recurring conversation for us is that we hardly go out of our way to develop relationships with other couples because we feel like we'll be saying good-bye in six months. We both have said we think the Phelpses and the Bodeens could be fun to get to know better. What if we had both couples over for a cookout on our patio?

Mary: We won't tell them that they are helping us save our marriage! I like that idea very much if we both work together to get ready and to do the cooking on the grill. It's just the sort of thing we need to do to show people we want to be good friends with them.

Ron: All right! And I'll get the grill ready so we can start the cooking in plenty of time before our friends arrive.

Pastor Cowan then presses Ron and Mary for a final commitment to two important details to make sure that there will be follow-through once they leave the counseling session.

Pastor: Your plans for your growth task sound good. But there are two details I didn't hear you mention: When will you have your friends over, and who will call to make the invitations?

Mary: I think two Saturdays from now around 5:00—what do you think, Ron? And I'll call the Phelpses, Ron, if you'll call the Bodeens. We can make those calls before our next meeting with Pastor Cowan.

Ron: That all sounds good to me. You've got yourself a deal!

Pastor: Now I have a final question. Are your plans realistic?

This exchange illustrates the most promising manner in which a couple can undertake a growth task before the final counseling session requiring new behavior in their relationship. Notice that Pastor Cowan did not even use the words "assignment" or "homework." It is important that the pastor help the couple design a task that is quite specific, such as Ron and Mary's planning to have two couples over and agreeing on a date and whom they will each call. Furthermore, it is essential that the pastor be sure that the growth task is realistic for the couple to undertake. It is important that the couple attempt new behavior in their marriage that is virtually assured of success.

Vague commitments such as "We'll be more understanding of each other this week," or "We'll have more fun together this week," while reflecting good intentions, will not be helpful. Such poorly defined plans do not offer people specific behaviors they need to adopt in order to fulfill their good intentions. Furthermore, tasks for action before the final session should involve both spouses equally and be rather brief. For example, Ron and Mary need only to consult their calendars when they return home, make plans for cleaning the house and grocery shopping, and then each make a phone call before the next counseling session. Whether or not they reduce their arguing, at least a couple can feel an important sense of accomplishment if, as in this case, they can report that they invited the other two couples, taking the first steps toward developing deeper friendships.

When the Counseling Session Appears Not to Go Well

It is entirely possible that a husband and wife will return to the second joint counseling session and say that nothing positive or encouraging has happened so far. There is always the chance that the old patterns of conflict are still occurring at home or perhaps even getting worse, and that each spouse has given up hope that the other will make any positive changes for the improvement of the marriage.

Severely conflicted couples can arrive at such a discouraging point largely because they have accumulated so much pain from long-standing frustrated needs and expectations. Constructive marital communication in such a tense context is difficult to achieve or maintain for most couples. The spouses become defensive and reactive to each other with little or no understanding for why each word they say widens the gulf between them and deepens the pain they feel. In such circumstances the counseling can surely appear to the pastor and to the couple not to be going very well at all. Certainly, the counseling with such troubled couples may not often sound as encouraging as that described in Pastor Cowan's work with the Nelsons.

However, even in a worst-case scenario it can be viewed as positive that the couple are still in the pastor's office, a point that may be appropriate to say to the couple. Despite all their conflicts, the couple are where they need to be to receive help or to be offered a referral to a specialist in marriage counseling. Indeed, a session that is filled with such conflict may in fact be looked back upon by the couple as a positive turning point, when they finally were directed to the professional help they had been avoiding for years! That is why such a tense session may only *appear* not to be going well.

Furthermore, the pastor enters each counseling session in this short-term process knowing that a referral may appropriately be made at any time. It is not necessary for the pastor to wait until the final session to make a referral. So it is entirely possible that a pastor may conclude midway through the second joint session that the couple cannot benefit any further from this short-term pastoral model, and that they need immediate attention from a specialist in marriage counseling. A pastor may offer this or a similar observation along with a referral:

> Pastor: Becky and Gary, as I have listened to each of you here, it seems that the more each of you talks the farther apart you get. I hear much pain and frustration from each of you. I doubt that either really feels heard by the other. This is not to say that I have given up hope for your marriage; that certainly isn't the case. However, I've concluded that you need more help than I can offer, and you will get better guidance if you work with a specialist in marriage counseling. I have referred a number of couples to Dr. Smith, a psychologist who specializes in helping couples like yourselves, and I respect Dr. Smith's work very much. I want to give you Dr. Smith's phone number, and I encourage you to call him tomorrow or the next day for an appointment as soon as possible. Which of you will make that call?

However, if at all possible, pastors are encouraged to affirm each of the spouses while preparing them to anticipate returning for the final joint session that was envisioned when the counseling began at the first joint session. While refusing to take sides, a pastor can greatly help each spouse by consistently hearing and restating the deepest feelings and concerns voiced by each spouse. Insisting that arguing spouses talk directly to the pastor instead of to each other can be an effective way to reduce defensive and reactive responses, while at the same time each spouse can hear perfectly well what the other is trying to express. A pastor may find it easier to cope with tense marital counseling sessions by remembering that *the primary goal of pastoral marriage counseling is to provide a context and a process in which both spouses can be heard and understood so both can then make their own best decisions for their marriage, their family, and themselves.* If a pastor can do marriage counseling from this viewpoint, there will be less anxiety about counseling sessions that appear to hold little or no promise for immediate resolution of deeply rooted and long-standing marital conflicts.

Even in such instances of persistent tension between spouses in the second joint session, the pastor can still invite them to consider what positive task or joint undertaking they might engage in together before the next and final counseling session. Once again, the pastor will avoid using the terms "homework" or "assignment." Couples can respond more readily to the suggestion that they try something together that they've never tried before, something that would ease the tension between them. Pastors might be very surprised by what a conflicted couple will consider. The possibilities could range all the way from, "Let's go to your mother's this weekend because we never fight in front of her," to "We can clean the garage together Saturday morning and not mention one word about our problems."

The willing undertaking of a single, joint task most certainly will not solve years of tension and arguing. But it can be a beginning, however small, for a couple to see that their relationship can hold something else for both of them besides endless and hopeless conflict. Pastoral marriage counseling is a hope-filled undertaking, and the pastor can invite the couple to try something new that might open their eyes a little bit to the possibility that they can effectively relate to each other in a more respectful and caring way while accomplishing something significant for their marriage. Furthermore, the couple will be more likely to be successful in accomplishing their task if the pastor has helped them to be very specific and concrete about what they intend to do together.

Ending the Second Joint Session

Before the session with both spouses comes to a close, the pastor should remind them that the next counseling session is the last session they had all agreed to, and that the primary aim of the final session is to assess all that has been accomplished and not accomplished in the total counseling process. In most instances, the pastor should allow an interval of at least a week or more between the second joint session and the final one. Time often permits persons to adopt a more conciliatory perspective if the differences are not too great. On the other hand, if the marriage problems continue to be severe or overwhelming at this point, it may be best for the couple to meet with the pastor within a week's time or sooner in order to consider what the next course of action should be.

After helping the couple to anticipate the next joint session, the pastor may choose to close with a prayer that recognizes and affirms the stress both spouses are feeling, acknowledges the presence and guidance of God's love, and asks for God's care to be with both spouses and with their family as they make important decisions.

Counseling Process in Stage 4 Session with Both Spouses

1. Possibly end counseling at the start of the session with a referral because of information the pastor has learned in the individual sessions.
2. Ask, "What things have you learned or feelings have you had in this counseling process or during your conversations with each other?"
3. Interrupt any attacking or blaming exchanges.
4. Ask, "What changes are you each prepared to make for your marriage?"
5. Ask, "What task(s) would you like to undertake together before the next session to help your marriage?"
6. Remind the couple that the next session will be the final session and will focus on an evaluation of what has been accomplished with the counseling.
7. Set an appointment for the next counseling session and close with a supportive prayer.

Preparation for the Final Counseling Session

Before the earlier individual sessions with each spouse, the pastor read the questionnaires from both persons and determined the principal issues to explore during the counseling sessions. The pastor should also prepare just as carefully for the final counseling session.

The Pastor's Written Evaluation of the Counseling Progress

Pastors will be much better prepared to meet the couple by thinking through and writing down their own responses to these four relationship assessment questions:

1. What are the specific problems that the husband and wife have said need to be resolved?
2. What other related or deeper issues must be taken into account with the original problems named by the spouses? What is the severity of those related issues?
3. What has realistically been accomplished so far in the counseling process toward the resolution of the couple's problems?
4. What are the necessary and appropriate actions that still need to be taken for all the main problems and issues in the marriage to be resolved satisfactorily for both spouses?

Engaging in this reflecting and writing process of preparation for the third joint session clarifies the pastor's own observations and thinking up to this point. Also, information may emerge during the final counseling session that will influence the pastor's conclusions. Of course, the views of the spouses are equally important. But by going through a process of organized and systematic reflection and writing before the final session, Pastor Cowan will be much better prepared to help Ron and Mary assess the progress they have made and the steps they need to take for greater harmony and satisfaction in their marriage.

Criteria for the Three Recommendation Options

In addition to the four couple assessment questions, pastors can be guided by certain criteria as they determine whether to encourage the ending of all counseling, make a referral to a community resource, or recontract with the couple for continued pastoral marriage counseling. Couples that are ready to end all counseling will usually fall into one of two groups:

1. Both spouses will agree that they have satisfactorily resolved the issue(s) or problem(s) that were causing them difficulty in their relationship. They will both be confident they can successfully work together on any other marital concerns that later come to their attention. They have significantly reduced their conflict, and they can focus on present and future issues without being distracted by each other's pain or distress about the relationship. Furthermore, they do not feel the need to engage in any further marriage counseling. Either spouse may want to follow through with individual counseling with another counselor, in which case further relationship issues may emerge later for the couple to examine together again.

2. One or both spouses will have decided that the marriage is over and that there is nothing further to be gained by more marriage counseling.

On the other hand, couples that might be considered by the pastor for one to three follow-up marriage counseling sessions will demonstrate the following:

1. They will have no continuing major relationship conflicts. They will be able to communicate and solve problems with each other without being sidetracked by past issues or emotional pain related to their marriage.
2. They will agree with the pastor's own observations and conclusion that they are now in a marriage growth mode that is hopeful and focused on the present and the future.
3. They will welcome and show evidence of benefiting from continued counseling support from their pastor, not requiring more than one to three more pastoral marriage counseling sessions for them to reach a satisfying, confident, and stable relationship. The further meetings with their pastor can serve to reinforce and integrate the new positive changes made in the marriage.

Likewise, the pastor will refer couples who essentially do not meet the above two sets of criteria to a professional marriage counselor. In other words, these are couples that will reflect one or more of the following:

1. They will be unresolved about one or more significant issues in their relationship, in many instances issues related to one or more of the ten "vital signs" or the three Tillichian polarized pairs of elements discussed in chapter 1.
2. One or both spouses will continue to experience painful emotions about past or current tensions and conflicts in their relationship.
3. They will find it difficult if not impossible to talk with each other without resorting to language and behavior that increase instead of decrease their conflict.
4. They will not feel confident that they have sufficient relationship and communication skills to resolve recurring disagreements.

These couples still need counseling help, but they will not receive the professional help they need through further counseling sessions with their pastor. The pastor may need to state this fact kindly but firmly to couples resistant to acknowledging their need for professional marriage counseling. Couples that clearly belong in this category should be referred by the pastor regardless of their expressed willingness or unwillingness to follow through with the referral. Besides, a referral declined today may be reconsidered next week or next month. Howard Stone is correct in his assertion that we cannot help everyone: "When certain parishioners do not respond to our best methods and efforts, we face the prospect of referral—but we cannot force parishioners into that, either. Ultimately we may need to let go and turn them over to God."[3]

The Process in the Final Counseling Session

Before the final session begins, the pastor not only should have reached tentative conclusions about the couple's progress but should also have decided how the session will be structured. The following outline will help to ensure a productive counseling session with the couple:

1. The pastor begins by inquiring how the husband and wife are presently relating to each other. It is essential for the pastor to know at the opening of the final session on what kind of terms the two spouses are dealing with each other at the moment.
2. The pastor states the primary purpose of the final session: to assess what has been accomplished and what the couple need to do for their marriage. The pastor also inquires if there are any matters that need *brief* attention in this counseling session.
3. Before beginning the assessment, the pastor should ask about the growth task that the couple had agreed to work on together. Did they accomplish the task or not? Did the couple learn anything from attempting the task or failing to complete it? (The pastor does not refer to the growth task as an assignment.)
4. The pastor and the couple make a careful assessment of the progress achieved as well as what has failed to be accomplished so far through the counseling.
5. The pastor and the couple reach conclusions together about the three options outlined at the beginning: (a) ending all counseling with this final session, (b) referring to another counseling source, or (c) recontracting for up to three more counseling sessions.
6. The pastor affirms the couple for investing in their marriage by completing the counseling process. The PMCQs are returned, and the pastor offers a closing prayer.

There should be no surprise to the couple about this outline for the final counseling session, because it reflects the original plan discussed and agreed to at the very first session. The process of the session, however, should be considered to be flexible. Although each point should somehow be included in the process of the session, varying amounts of time, as needed, may be spent at any point during the session. Sometimes more time will be given to the assessment phase, and on other occasions more time will be needed for dealing with the growth task from the previous session or for discussing the pastor's recommendation of a referral to another counselor. The timing and pacing of each step of the process with periodic reference to the clock will necessarily be on the pastor's mind to ensure that all the necessary elements are adequately addressed within the counseling hour. The following excerpts of counseling dialogue show how a pastor may follow the structured process for the session.

1. *Checking out present feelings.* After greeting Mary and Ron, Pastor Cowan invites them to sit down, again in chairs arranged so each person can see the other two with equal ease. Then Pastor Cowan pointedly asks, "Just as I did the last time we started, I want a weather report from each of you describing the emotional state between the two of you at the moment." Pastor Cowan then waits for each of them to offer a description of the feeling tone between them as they begin this last session. The pastor is not surprised if there is some incongruence between the two reports, since husband and wife always hold, at any given moment, two different perspectives on their relationship.

While being very important, this initial step in the last session should take only a few minutes. Only in a crisis situation would a reported stormy mood between the spouses require major attention in the session before making an effort toward assessment and pastoral recommendations.

2. *Defining the purpose of the session.* After inquiring briefly about the present status of the couple's relationship, the pastor states what is to be accomplished in the counseling session.

> Pastor: Ron and Mary, when you began this marriage counseling process several weeks ago, we agreed that the purpose of this particular session would be mainly for assessment and evaluation of what has been accomplished for your marriage and what still remains to be done. In the light of that assessment, we can consider what the best courses of action should be, including the possibility of any further counseling. So after I hear from you about the growth task you promised to work on

during the past week, I suggest we move right to the assessment. Does that agree with your understanding of the purpose for this session?

If the pastor fails to state the purpose of the session right at the outset, the direction can easily be lost or go astray. Particularly if there is a high level of tension or disagreement between the spouses, the focus of the session can readily be diverted to the issues of conflict and the original goal for assessment be lost in the process. The pastor will also ask if either partner wants to put any other items on the agenda in addition to the assessment process.

> Pastor: Besides evaluating what has been accomplished and what still needs to be achieved for your marriage, are there any other concerns that either of you would like us to discuss?
>
> Mary: Yes, I just need to say that when I brought in the mail today I saw a letter for Ron that came from the director of the branch office where Ron turned down the job offer. My stomach turned a flip, because I imagined the director was writing to beg Ron to change his mind. Ron didn't say anything about the letter, and I'd like to just get it clarified and then I can put my mind on our purpose for this session.
>
> Pastor: Sure, we can talk about that for a few minutes before we do the assessing. But I don't want us to take too much time away from the time for the assessment.
>
> Mary: That's fine. I'll just feel better if Ron can assure me again of his commitment to the plans we are making for our family right here where we live now.

The purpose of the final session is now fully understood by the pastor and the couple. Mary's concern can be dealt with briefly before the assessment process without jeopardizing the main focus for the counseling session. Even if Mary's concern begins to open up old and tense issues between Mary and Ron, the attention of the session must be returned to assessment.

3. *Reviewing the growth task.* The couple's experience in completing their growth task can be another gauge for the pastor's evaluation of the strength of the marital relationship and progress made through counsel-

ing. However, the pastor must be careful about drawing any firm conclusions from what the couple reports. In many instances couples will likely say that they did not have much success with their intended task, no matter how realistic and concrete the plans they had made. Pastors can expect that couples with severe conflicts will hardly ever attempt, let alone complete, the task they agreed to undertake. Even couples who are making good progress may or may not handle their growth task successfully. But in those instances when the couple completes their growth task, this can often be regarded as a step toward significant progress in their relationship.

The pastor can ask questions to help the couple evaluate their work together on their growth task.

What did you learn or discover as you worked together?

What was the hardest part for you to do?

What did you enjoy the most?

Were some of the problems you encountered in doing this task typical in any respect to the problems you have had in other areas of your marriage?

What would be the next appropriate growth task you should undertake to continue making progress in your marriage?

4. *Assessing progress made through counseling.* Pastor Cowan wisely remembers that it is not her responsibility to offer her conclusions at the beginning of the assessment. She introduces the assessment by inviting the Nelsons to offer their own evaluations of what they feel has been accomplished through the marriage counseling process. Pastor Cowan also uses this occasion to affirm the Nelsons for their commitment to see the counseling through to the final session.

Pastor: Mary and Ron, I congratulate you for beginning and staying with this counseling process to the end! Now we have come to the central purpose for this session as we evaluate what has been achieved and what still remains to be done so you both can feel better about your marriage. I expect there will be agreement about some areas of improvement, but also that you each may see some things differently. Let's begin with each of you saying what you feel has been accomplished since this counseling process began.

The process of evaluation can offer the couple a good opportunity for understanding better the sources of conflict in their marriage. Because the focus of the evaluation is necessarily upon the past four or more weeks instead of the past several years, observations can be more specific and accurate, and each spouse can more easily recall events referred to by the other. It is easier and more productive to discuss the causes and dynamics of an argument that is only two weeks old than a conflict that occurred two years ago.

However, it is also more than likely that the couple's principal conflicts over the years have surfaced and been evident in the interactions of the preceding weeks. Certain patterns of interaction for a conflicted couple usually do not change much over the years. For example, a couple that has always had difficulty finding quality time for communication will very likely have had somehow to deal with that issue after beginning the pastoral marriage counseling. Or a couple that generally disagrees on how to handle money will most likely have had at least some occasions in the past month for facing that issue. Assessment of their relationship since beginning the counseling will very likely help most couples examine the most conflicted areas of their marriage. Of course, if a troubled couple engages in longer term counseling with another professional, there will likely be other sources and aspects of marital conflict that will later come to light.

A pastor is encouraged to be a bit skeptical about reports from spouses that extraordinary or remarkable progress has occurred in dealing with their marriage problems. As a rule, marriages do not get into trouble overnight, and rarely do enormous changes for the better occur quickly. Of course, it is very gratifying if a couple declares that all problems have been resolved in the space of four to six weeks of counseling. However, a pastor would be wise to keep in mind that real growth in even the best of marriages is a slow process. That is not to say that a month or two months of counseling cannot make an enormous difference in changing the course of a marriage, but in most marriages intentional and determined work will still be required of both spouses if the changes for the better are to be continued.

A realistic and honest approach is the best attitude for both the pastor and the couple to evaluate any recent changes for the better the couple can identify in their relationship.

> Mary: There is no question that Ron and I have talked more with each other in the past four weeks than we have in the past four years. I've seen Ron so preoccupied with his job and I've been

so involved with the kids that we were like two ships passing in the night. Now, at least, we are talking. I have a husband back!

Ron: I think that this counseling process has helped us to get some priorities sorted and straightened out for our marriage and for our family. Not only were we two ships passing, but we were starting to head off in different directions, and that was getting scary for me. I'm committed to Mary, and I have no doubt about Mary's commitment to me. That's a big accomplishment for us in the past month!

Mary: The fact that we decided to have some friends over next week for a cookout is also a major accomplishment for us. It may not seem like a big deal to anyone else, but we haven't entertained for three years. I feel really good that we said we are going to do it and that we each called and offered an invitation this past week!

Ron: By planning for that patio party, we actually reaffirmed that we can work on some things together and have fun. That really feels good!

The pastor should affirm the couple for all that they have accomplished. But it is not time yet for the pastor to offer observations and conclusions about the couple's relationship. The pastor should ask the couple to continue explaining further not only what they have accomplished but also what areas—with each other and with their relationship—they now recognize more clearly still need work.

Pastor: I am wondering now what you both feel needs more attention so that your marriage can be more nearly what both of you want for yourselves and for your family.

Ron: Well, as much as we might change at home, it's still a demanding and sometimes heartless world out there. Corporations ask for loyalty, but they aren't loyal to their employees unless their employees produce. That worries me all the time. I know that I have a long way to go so my life, our marriage, and our family don't get all twisted out of shape because of my work.

Mary: Having some friends over for a cookout on our patio is the easy part. I think it will be a greater challenge for all of us if I start spending some time outside the home at a part-time job or with some community activities. I know it will mean changes in how we do things, because I won't be able to do all the work I do now in the home if I'm outside the home fifteen or more hours a week. Those changes and what they might mean to our marriage worry me.

Only after both spouses have had the opportunity to say at length how they see the accomplishments and the areas needing further work should the pastor consider making observations from a pastoral perspective about the marriage. The spouses will be much more open to hearing the pastor's thoughts after they have offered theirs. The pastor will wisely take into account everything that the couple has just said while also acknowledging and affirming the strengths in the couple's marriage.

Pastor: I believe that I have reached conclusions similar to what both of you have described. I am impressed with your commitment to each other and to your marriage. You really do care about each other in a very loving way, and you really want to work together! I think you're a great team! I also saw pretty much the same areas for continued growth as you did. Ron, it can be very tough to come to grips with all the inner voices and instincts that drive one to survive at work. And Mary, I think you stated it well about the changes you and Ron and your family will be facing as you find work or activities that take you out of the home. I agree with what I think both of you are sensing, that there are many challenges still ahead for your marriage.

5. *Making recommendations and referrals.* If their marital problems are in the early stages, many couples will benefit from the short-term marriage counseling process. Sometimes a couple will be ready to end the marriage counseling with the final session, and both the couple and the pastor will feel that their problems are under control. Other couples will end the counseling without a strong sense of accomplishment, but with a determination to tolerate their problems in the future as they have in the past.

If the couple desires further counseling with the pastor, the pastor should respond carefully. *A basic guideline in most circumstances is for a pastor to see a couple for no more than three joint sessions beyond the final session of this short-term model.* A pastor who is not in a specialized counseling ministry and who chooses to go beyond ten formal counseling sessions with a couple (which include this short-term model) should examine carefully the rationale and personal motivations for such an extended commitment to the couple. That is not to say that longer-term pastoral counseling is always inappropriate, but in the context of the varied demands and responsibilities of the parish and the particular challenges and demands of longer-term counseling, such extended commitments to pastoral counseling should be very carefully evaluated. Most often, a good referral to another counselor can be the best expression of responsible pastoral care. If, however, the pastor arranges with the couple for the first of the possibly three follow-up marriage counseling sessions, the pastor is referred to the final section in chapter 5 and to appendix E.

Usually parishioners will respond positively to their pastor's referral if it is to a professional with whom the pastor has a personal acquaintance and in whom the pastor has obvious confidence. If a pastor says to a distraught parishioner, "I recommend that you see a psychiatrist for your depression," in most instances the parishioner is not likely to follow through on the referral. But if a pastor can say, "I recommend that you see Dr. Green at the medical center. I know Dr. Green and have referred others to her and have felt good about her care for those people," the parishioner is much more likely to act on the recommendation.

It is equally important for a pastor not to overrate the person to whom the parishioner is being referred. To say, "Dr. Green has been very successful with everyone I have ever sent to her, and I am sure that she is exactly the person for you so you will never be depressed again," is to do a disservice to both the parishioner and to Dr. Green. A parishioner given unrealistic assurances often will not continue with the new professional person because the "miracle cure" does not happen as the parishioner had been led to expect. Obviously, for a pastor to be able to make effective referrals, it is necessary to make every effort to become well acquainted with the professional counseling and mental health resources in the community and surrounding area. Furthermore, parishioners will find it helpful if a pastor has business cards to hand out along with the referral.

When a pastor makes a referral to another professional, in most all instances it is far better for parishioners to make their own initial appointments. By observing that practice, parishioners are allowed to take responsibility for their own well-being, and the pastor avoids the professional embarrassment of a parishioner failing to show up for an appointment the pastor has made. In fact, many professional offices will not even accept an attempt by someone else to make an appointment for another person.

When working with a couple and making recommendations or referrals in the final joint session, it is important for the pastor to be guided by the *principle of balance* so neither spouse is put in the position of appearing to be the main source of the marital conflict. In other words, the pastor tries not to single out just one spouse for further professional counseling or care. In the earlier example, balance will be maintained if Pastor Cowan refers Ron to a support group for men, Mary to a support group for women, and both together to a marriage counselor.

Without there being near balance in the recommendations, one spouse may unjustly conclude that the other spouse is "sicker" and the obvious cause of all the marital stress. Unless there is shared responsibility for a marriage and for the conflicts in the relationship, there is little possibility for those conflicts to be happily and constructively resolved. However, in the cases of alcohol or chemical abuse or marital violence, the "using" or "abusing" spouse must take full responsibility for his or her own abusive behavior. It is never the other spouse's fault that a spouse abuses alcohol or chemicals or engages in violent behavior. If a respectful and trusting marital relationship is recovered despite previous abuse, there will need to be a commitment by both spouses to working together on their new relationship, often with the help of an ongoing support group for each spouse.

In many circumstances a pastor may have a recommendation or referral for each spouse as well as a recommendation or referral for them together. If either spouse is surprised by the recommendations or resistant to the pastor's suggestions, a discussion of those reservations may help that person accept the recommendations.

6. *Ending the session and counseling process.* The couple has just concluded an important investment they have made together toward reconciliation and the enhancement of their marriage. The pastor should affirm the couple for their commitment to the counseling and to their marriage. Finally, before offering a closing prayer that asks for God's continuing care of the couple and their family, the pastor will return to the couple their Pastoral Marriage Counseling Questionnaires. The pastor may also wish to tell the couple that the pastor has not retained any notes or papers from the counseling sessions, thus assuring them that their privacy and confidentiality have been protected.

Final Session: Preparation and Process

1. Written preparation
   a. What are the specific problems stated by the couple?
   b. Are there any other related issues?
   c. What realistically has been accomplished?
   d. What actions are necessary to resolve the problems and issues?
2. Counseling process
   a. Check out present relating.
   b. Define the purpose of the session.
   c. Review the growth task.
   d. Assess progress.
   e. Make recommendations.
   f. Affirm the couple, return PMCQs, and close with prayer.

Continuing Pastoral Care

The process of short-term pastoral marriage counseling takes place within the larger context of general pastoral care and the church's ministry to persons. As parishioners, the partners remain within the pastoral oversight and responsibility of the pastor, even if one or both spouses are referred to another mental health professional. In the best of circumstances a pastor will know of such professionals in the community to whom parishioners can be referred, and a working relationship—with the counselee's permission—can be established between the other professional and the pastor. When a parishioner has been referred to another counselor, the pastor's proper role is to continue normal pastoral contact and care but not to establish or maintain an ongoing counseling relationship with the church member.

In the cases where a couple happily ends the marriage counseling process, continuing pastoral care should include a follow-up visit in the couple's home within two months to see how the couple is doing. If it should become apparent in the course of the visit that there are further marital issues to be worked on, the pastor should consider scheduling an appointment at the church office within the next week instead of renewing counseling in the couple's home.

Conclusion

The purpose of the brief marriage counseling model is to offer a realistic plan for both pastor and spouses for intervention in a conflicted marriage. When the pastor and the couple have agreed to follow the process that has been outlined, they then have a procedure for gathering essential information, exploring the sources of conflict, and committing to new courses of action toward resolution. Moreover, the plan will lead to a definite ending point for assessment and recommendations so the couple can take the necessary steps toward resolving troubling problems. Throughout the counseling process, the pastor's role is not that of an expert marriage counselor, though in many instances pastors are quite skilled in their counseling methods. Rather, the pastor's primary role and authority are defined by the pastoral office and rooted in the pastoral care tradition of the church. Utilizing the brief marriage counseling model within the context of their pastoral office and authority, pastors can now confidently offer a promising plan to conflicted couples. And countless couples who might otherwise not find any help at all, through faithful pastoral guidance, God's assured presence, and the miracle of heartfelt dialogue, will be empowered to take hope-filled steps toward marital reconciliation, growth, and renewal.

Chapter Five

The Plan for Counseling Challenges

Marriage is a risk even when the couple have known each other from childhood. It is an attempt to bridge the gap between the solitariness of me and the solitariness of you. It is born of basic needs on several levels of personality—from the biological need for sexual union to the psychological need for intimacy to the spiritual need to care intensely about another human being's welfare. When such basic need systems become interrelated, it is natural that there will be both attraction and repulsion. The one I love I also hate at times.

—Charles William Stewart,
The Minister as Marriage Counselor (1970 ed.)

This chapter covers:

- ~ What to do when the plan seems not to be working
- ~ Professional support and supervision
- ~ Mandated reporting
- ~ Avoiding a sexist bias
- ~ Cross-cultural dialogue
- ~ Professional boundaries
- ~ Children of conflicted marriages
- ~ Sexual problems
- ~ Responding to domestic violence
- ~ When divorce is the choice
- ~ Further counseling sessions

When Pastor Cowan gathers her courage to sit in the same room and try to care for two people who are alternating back and forth between love and hate for each other, she soon discovers that pastoral marriage counseling is a very challenging undertaking. But because Pastor Cowan is a professional person, she will anticipate and plan for as many of those challenges as possible, and thereby reduce her chances of being caught unprepared without an adequate plan for the couple and for the counseling process. The purpose of this chapter is to help Pastor Cowan prepare for some of the most likely and most difficult problems she can encounter as a pastoral marriage counselor.

When This Plan Seems Not to Be Working

This model for short-term pastoral marriage counseling does not promise to solve all troubled marriages, although it offers a responsible and faithful pastoral response. Therefore, *even in the face of very conflicted marriages and difficult counseling situations when the plan seems not to be working, pastors are strongly encouraged not to abandon this basic model.*

Perhaps the greatest temptation for many pastors will be to do counseling by following their parishioners' resistance instead of leading as a guide who can see a promising trail ahead. Instead of stating clearly that the best way for him or her to be helpful is through following the plan, the pastor may instead let the parishioners design and lead the direction of the counseling. This kind of departure from the plan might happen, for example, if a husband and wife insist, and the pastor agrees, to be seen several times separately before the initial joint session. Another significant deviation from the plan would be for the pastor to agree to counseling sessions that go well over an hour in length. If a pastor does not make a referral to another professional marriage counselor and agrees to work with the couple outside the guidelines of this plan for short-term pastoral marriage counseling, then that pastor will be sharply limiting the possibilities for being a positive and truly helpful resource to a troubled couple. If parishioners are resistant to the marriage counseling plan and also refuse to consider a referral to another counseling resource, then it is best for a pastor not to attempt marriage counseling but instead to continue routine pastoral care contacts.

Professional Support and Supervision

Ron and Mary Nelson would be very fortunate if their pastor made the following phone call to another pastor the morning after meeting with them for the first time.

Pastor Cowan:Hi, Howard? I'm glad I caught you in the office before you started on your hospital calls. Well, it's my turn this time to call our pastoral counseling support group to a meeting. I saw a couple for marriage counseling last night for the first time, and I'm going to be doing some short-term counseling work with them. I'd like to present their case to the group for insight and feedback. I hope you can make it to our meeting next Friday. We're scheduled to meet at St. Andrew's.

Ron and Mary Nelson would have reason to be very grateful, because their pastor takes her counseling work so seriously that she took the leadership initiative with another pastor and helped form a pastoral counseling support group with five other pastors in order to share counseling cases with each other. By following a case study method that protects the counselees' personal identity, the pastors can outline the dynamics of a counseling situation along with issues and concerns for which they feel they need better understanding. Furthermore, in every professional discipline, discussing one's practices and procedures in a case study format is perhaps the best way possible for avoiding lapses of professional judgment that could lead to serious consequences for the persons being served. Therefore, it is essential for pastors to recognize, as Pastor Cowan does, that there is much they can do themselves to create and establish a peer support group to meet their own professional needs.

Involvement in other people's intense, emotional crises can easily evoke strong feelings in both the pastor and the counselee toward each other. The occurrence of a wide range of feelings in the pastor and counselees is very natural and cannot be avoided. As human beings, pastors may experience any range of emotional responses to counselees, including but not limited to anger, envy, impatience, superiority, intimidation, anxiety, and sexual attraction. However, if the behaviors prompted by those feelings, particularly the pastor's behaviors, are not properly reviewed by peers, a consultant, or a supervisor, and are not appropriately managed, the counseling process can be unhelpful or even damaging for the parishioner. Miller and Jackson have stated the issue succinctly:

> These reactions are particularly dangerous when they happen to fit into a pattern of transference from the client, as when a dependent client finds a therapist with rescue needs, or a seductive client finds a counselor with a strong need to be admired and loved. Every counselor sets out with the fantasy that "It could never happen to me,"

but many become ensnared in these difficult situations. Where a pastoral role is involved, such relationships can further evolve into emotional or even financial blackmail and the potential loss of parish and profession.[1]

Every experienced counselor is always carefully monitoring her or his own emotional responses while keeping a primary focus on the counseling process and what is in the counselee's best interests. Counseling both partners of a marriage does not necessarily lessen the possibility for the pastor's own feelings to become a hindrance to the counseling process. Indeed, the pastoral involvement with two persons in a single counseling relationship can increase the possibility for the pastor's viewpoint and behavior to become distracted and distorted. Therefore, *it is a wise pastor who intentionally creates a viable support system with other professional persons for reviewing pastoral counseling cases and for knowing the best resources in the community for referral.*

In most parish settings, it will take only a little imaginative thinking for a pastor to locate and to make use of other willing professional resource persons. Many physicians, social workers, or psychologists will welcome an inquiry from a pastor who, for example, would like to review counseling concerns over lunch once a month. Often a pastor can make such an informal arrangement at no cost or fee. Likewise, a group of pastors meeting regularly to discuss counseling cases might find a physician or other counseling professional who would be glad for the opportunity to meet with the pastors as their consulting resource at no cost. One may feel it is risky to have one's counseling judgments and practices viewed by professional colleagues, but what can be learned for the benefit of one's parishioners more than makes any possible risk worthwhile.

An important question is whether interprofessional consultation violates the confidentiality of parishioners. A pastor is always correct to be sure that the details of people's lives shared in the office or study remain confidential. With that concern in mind, a pastor has two options when seeking consultation from other professional persons. One possibility is for the pastor to tell counselees about his or her wish to discuss their situation with another professional person and to secure their written permission to do this. Another alternative is simply to disguise names and identifying data and discuss only the essential case dynamics without informing the counselees that any outside consultation is taking place. Whatever steps the pastor takes, the parishioners' right to confidentiality must be protected. However, it is always a wise act on the part of the pastor to seek professional consultation so that the parishioners receive the best help possible.

Increasingly, more clinical training opportunities are available to pastors through church-related agencies and pastoral counseling centers. The American Association of Pastoral Counselors (AAPC) encourages the continued training of clergy in the disciplines of pastoral counseling. The AAPC has several levels of affiliation and membership, and has set standards for the clinical training of pastors in the basic skills of counseling. Pastors are urged to seek out the professional persons in their area who are associated with the AAPC and also participate in training programs that meet AAPC standards.[2] An additional resource is the American Association for Marriage and Family Therapy (AAMFT). The AAMFT sets clinical standards for a membership comprised of marriage and family therapists in many disciplines, including social workers, psychologists, and clinically trained clergy. By contacting the national office of the AAMFT, a pastor can locate AAMFT members in one's area who could be approached and considered for possible referrals or as a consulting resource for the pastor.[3]

Mandated Reporting of the Abuse of Children and Vulnerable Adults

Pastors never know when in the course of pastoral care or counseling they may learn of instances of alleged abuse of children or vulnerable adults. All clergy should know the local, county, or state requirements for them to report to the appropriate authorities evidence of possible physical or sexual abuse of children or of vulnerable adults. Within the social services area or division there should be an office for child protection and abuse reporting as well as an office for reporting adult abuse. A pastor can easily find out from those offices exactly what the law expects of clergy. A pastor wanting written clarification can request a copy of the relevant legal statute mandating clergy reporting.

Pastors should not be surprised in the course of counseling to learn of a situation in a home that sounds like it could possibly be abusive. But there may be complicating or extenuating circumstances that cause the pastor to wonder whether reporting a situation is warranted. Some pastors may rightly discuss a possible abusive situation with a counseling consultant or a group of pastors meeting to discuss counseling cases. Ordinarily, local government offices will welcome a telephone call from a pastor who wants to review a situation with a caseworker without giving any names or identifying information about the persons involved. In this way a pastor can learn authoritatively whether or not a situation fits the criteria for being reported. If the case is one that should be reported, then the pastor must make the decision whether to call back and report names and details about the alleged abuse.

It is becoming increasingly common for a pastor to be required to report instances of abuse within twenty-four hours of learning of the abuse, with a written report to follow within seventy-two hours. Requirements for mandated reporting can vary from state to state, which is all the more reason why a pastor should make sure to inquire about the actual legal requirements where the pastor lives.[4]

Clergy may feel uncomfortable about any requirement to report a church family or individual parishioner where there is evidence of abuse. Many clergy will claim the "seal of the confessional," meaning that any information reported to them in confidence must never be divulged, under any circumstances, to a court or other civil authority. Furthermore, in many instances, clergy know that they run the almost certain risk of alienating a family or members of a family if the pastor turns in their names to a government office.

On the other hand, *a pastor must remember that the primary issue at stake is always the safety and well-being of a vulnerable child or a vulnerable adult.* In most instances, if there is no civil or law enforcement intervention, the abuse of a child or an adult is most likely to continue and perhaps even get worse. Furthermore, if a situation of unreported child or adult abuse does eventually come to the attention of authorities, there is always the possibility that someone will say that she or he had reported the abuse situation to the pastor. Then the pastor may have some serious and embarrassing questions to answer for not reporting the abuse at that time.

Pastors will be in a position to make the best professional and pastoral decisions when they have consulted directly with civil or governmental authorities about the specific legal requirements and expectations of clergy who have learned of the sexual or physical abuse of a child or a vulnerable adult. And there is always the distinct possibility, if a pastor finds it necessary to report a parishioner for child or adult abuse, that the pastor may be surprised by the gratitude of family members that at last a tragic secret in their family has come to the attention of the proper authorities.

Avoiding a Sexist Bias

No persons are without biases that can influence at any time their responses to others. It is unfortunate for counselees and parishioners when a pastor is not aware of personal biases, resulting in unhelpful or even denigrating and belittling observations or comments. Pastors are especially vulnerable to making such serious counseling errors when they assume that they understand well the needs and concerns of persons of the opposite sex.

The Swiss psychiatrist Paul Tournier very wisely observed, "I will go so far as to say that never can a man completely understand a woman, nor a woman a man."[5] This conclusion clearly applies to marital dynamics as well as to the professional practice of clergy counseling parishioners of the opposite sex. Even what seem to be the most casual comments can betray an offensive sexist bias. Men referring to adult women as "girls" or commenting on their mental capacity is never appropriate or acceptable. Likewise, women suggesting that men never ask for directions or change the toilet paper roll are just as out of place.

We should be especially careful here not to consider this issue to be one merely of so-called political correctness. The primary issue for the pastoral counselor is one of valuing the unique experience of each parishioner and counselee. Donald Capps has pointedly addressed this matter in the final chapter of his book *Giving Counsel: A Minister's Guidebook*. Capps asserts that in order to provide counsel, pastors need a judicious frame of mind. He adds that a judicious frame of mind has two qualities—namely, treating others with kindness and valuing their uniqueness. On the latter quality he writes:

> When the minister provides counsel, she should not focus on how Bill or Emily do or do not fit universal or group norms, but on the "organization" woven from the universal, group, and idiosyncratic characteristics that make Bill or Emily the unique persons they are. When we mourn the loss of a loved one, we mourn the passing of a person who was *sui generis*, one of a kind. It is perfectly true—not just hyperbole or exaggeration—when the mourners say to one another, "We will not see the likes of him-or-her again."[6]

Obviously, any sexist bias on the part of the pastor does not value the uniqueness of the other person.

This is why it is essential for pastors to realize that when they deal with persons of the opposite sex, they are really doing cross-cultural counseling; they are observers of another culture quite distinct from the culture of their own sexual identity. While his book *Pastoral Counseling across Cultures* examines issues mainly related to geographically distinct cultures, David Augsburger's study is also particularly informative for its treatment of the culturally different worldview between women and men. Speaking of what he calls "interpathic caring," Augsburger notes:

> I, the culturally different, seek to learn and fully entertain within my consciousness a foreign belief. I take a foreign perspective, base my thought on a foreign assumption, and allow myself to feel the resultant feelings and their cognitive and emotive consequences in my personality as I inhabit, insofar as I am capable of inhabiting, a foreign context.[7]

The importance of Augsburger's method is underscored by Carol Gilligan's observation that men and women do not even speak the same language:

> My research suggests that men and women may speak different languages that they assume are the same, using similar words to encode disparate experiences of self and social relationships. Because these languages share an overlapping moral vocabulary, they contain a propensity for systematic mistranslation, creating misunderstandings which impede communication and limit the potential for cooperation and care in relationships.[8]

So the pastoral counselor, whether female or male, never forgets how profoundly unique are the disparate experiences of men and women. While some of our understandings of men and women may be generally accurate, we must never forget that we are always foreigners eavesdropping on another culture when we try to understand the concerns and issues of persons of the opposite sex. Thus, it will be with the utmost respect, and with a sense of awe, that the pastoral counselor goes about the task and challenge of trying to understand the personal experiences of both a husband and a wife.

For these reasons, the pastoral counselor also should never lose sight of the obvious fact that in marriage counseling there are always two persons of the same sex in the counseling room—and the pastor is always in the majority! In many if not most counseling situations, the sexual imbalance in the room will not be a strong negative factor for the spouse in the minority. But the pastor should never assume that the imbalance is not an issue. Most certainly the sexual imbalance is a block to effective counseling if the pastor takes the side of the spouse of the same sex. Male clergy are particularly susceptible to contributing to such an imbalance if they hold the view that the wife is supposed to do her husband's bidding. *It is the pastor's responsibility and task to demonstrate consistently that both spouses are human beings equally loved by God and therefore of equal worth and dignity in the marriage.* This essential message will undergird all else that occurs in the counseling process, and will be completely dependent upon the counselor's wholehearted theological, attitudinal, and behavioral commitment to a nonsexist bias.

Cross-Cultural Dialogue

Culture is like the air we breathe. We are utterly dependent upon it, and we hardly pay it any attention until we suddenly encounter a new odor.[9] Because we so easily take our culture for granted, we are hardly if at all aware how much of our own culture shapes our perceptions and responses to our world. It is particularly dismaying how easily our own culture can assume a sense of superiority when another culture is encountered. This is why pastors must be especially sensitive toward the increasing numbers of persons who have come to this country themselves or whose parents came as immigrants. We live in an increasingly multicultural society, with those who are white and non-Hispanic projected to represent only slightly more than half of the population in this country by 2050.[10] Likewise, a white, middle-class, heterosexual pastor will be meeting other distinct cultures from within our own country when seeking to help persons of color, gay or lesbian persons, blue-collar laborers, and persons with less than a college education.[11]

Pastoral marriage counselors can be much more effective if they keep in mind Howard Clinebell's observation:

> In working with persons from different ethnic, cultural, or sexual backgrounds, it is essential to be aware of the universal tendency to feel, on some level, that one's own experiences and culture are the norm for all human beings. . . . When counseling with a person from a different gender or cultural background, it is helpful to say: "I realize that, much as I would like to understand what you are saying, I won't understand at times because of the differences in our backgrounds. Our work together will be more helpful if you will tell me when you sense I'm not really understanding what you are saying."[12]

Therefore, the culturally sensitive pastor will try all the harder to hear counselees as they define and explain their issues and concerns in terms of their own cultural framework. Though the cultural and ethnic differences between the pastor and the counselee may be readily apparent, the underlying relationship issues will still often match well with the marriage dynamics discussed in chapter 1.

Professional Boundaries

Addressing ethics in ministry, Walter Wiest and Elwyn Smith make this important observation:

> Without distance, compassion is corrupted. A mature professional does not see compassion as constrained by distance. Psychological distance actually gives room for the labors of compassion and protects both the counselee and the pastor from forces that threaten to falsify professional service. A mature professional possesses the ability to project concern that unites compassion with appropriate distance.[13]

However, many pastors think the notions of compassion and distance are mutually exclusive, that both cannot be brought together in the responsible practice of professional ministry. In fact, some pastors feel that the artificial maintenance of distance will intrude upon an authentic, caring ministry. Such a view would more readily describe the pastor as a "friend" instead of a professional. Indeed, the widespread practice of referring to clergy by their first name, as "Pastor Julie" or "Pastor Phil," suggests the pastor is virtually a member of each of the families in the parish with hardly more distance between pastor and parishioners than family members customarily observe with each other.

It is no secret among clergy, their parishioners, and even the non-church-going public that clergy have too often misused their positions of power for their sexual benefit at the violation and expense of their parishioners and counselees. In every one of those instances, a pastor purposely or unwittingly crossed over a boundary marking the difference between appropriate and inappropriate professional behavior.[14]

Professional ministry is exactly that! Professionals are paid to provide a service, and the service provided defines the essential focus of the relationship. Likewise, professional ministry provides a service, for which in most instances there is even a written contract. The primary purpose of parish ministry is not for a pastor to develop friendships, though such friendships may occur. No matter how warm, cordial, and friendly a pastor-parishioner relationship may be, it is first, foremost, and always a professional relationship. And regardless of whether or not parishioners remember the relationship is always professional, it is always the responsibility of pastors to remember that the relationship with their parishioners is first of all professional. As a result, pastors must always be thinking about professional boundaries no matter the situation where they are involved with parishioners.[15]

The consideration of appropriate pastoral boundaries should naturally come to mind in a variety of settings that typically occur in parish ministry. After all, pastors are discreet about respecting parishioners' privacy in a hospital setting. Parishioners may attempt to engage in counseling sessions over the telephone, which will be discouraged by the responsible pastor who will set an appointment for counseling in his or her office. Likewise, pastoral boundaries are observed by time-limited counseling sessions and home visits.

Equally important is the observance of responsible pastoral boundaries regarding the touching of parishioners. Most parishioners will feel relief and assurance when they instinctively realize that their pastor has clear boundaries about not touching them. Parishioners need to know that when they are vulnerable or in a private setting with their pastor they will not be touched. This is to say that if a pastor thinks that an arm placed on a parishioner's shoulder or a hug is appropriate, it always occurs in the presence of others. *There is never any justification for a pastor to initiate a hug during or following a counseling session.*

The short-term marriage counseling model obviously has numerous built-in professional boundaries, such as a prescribed number of sessions, all typically completed in meetings fifty to sixty minutes in length. The short-term model is necessarily defined by essential boundaries, and presumes that a responsible pastoral intervention in troubled marriages requires professional boundaries. Parishioners will recognize and respect their pastor's observance of professional boundaries, which will help most parishioners feel more secure and confident about the counseling process.

The Children of Conflicted Marriages

According to a national survey, over half of all children of elementary school age interviewed said they feel afraid when their parents have arguments.[16] Children of any age readily sense the levels of tension between their parents. Children may not hear all the words or understand the issues, but they certainly can feel very deeply the emotional and disruptive impact of long-standing alienation between their parents. Even more disturbing is the toll that marital abuse can take on children who are the most vulnerable where violence is occurring. Forty to 60 percent of men who abuse women also abuse children.[17]

The counseling pastor cannot ignore the children who are the emotional victims of their parents' fighting. Andrew Lester has rightly declared that pastors have a critical responsibility for making sensitive interventions in the lives of troubled children.

> We know that many of the emotional, relational, and spiritual problems with which adults suffer result from childhood crises that were not resolved creatively. Effective pastoral care with a child in crisis may prevent the crisis from having a lifelong debilitating effect on the child's emotional, physical, and spiritual health.[18]

Some parents will ask whether children are affected by marital conflict or divorce, a reasonable question in light of the estimate that 38 percent of children born to married parents will experience divorce before age 16.[19] The answer is always yes, even at risk to be seriously affected into adulthood as Judith Wallerstein has reported.[20] Frequently, parents in conflicted marriages are concerned whether their children will have serious behavioral problems or in other troubling ways not adjust presently, or in the future, to the emotional and even abusive stress in the home.

Whether or not children have obvious adjustment problems, all children are affected by continuing conflict between their parents. The question is not whether children are affected by parental strife, but to what *degree* they are affected. Indeed, many children cope with the emotional strain of family tensions by being model students in school and church. Through outstanding academic or athletic achievement, young people can create a substitute environment of support and affirmation in place of what is threatened and unavailable to them in a family upset by continuing parental conflict. Reports of children having trouble at school, or indications through a child's behavior problems at church, can be clear tip-offs that a child most likely is not coping effectively with the marital problems at home. However, in every instance where a couple with children is having serious marital problems, the pastor will always be correct in assuming that the children are personally faced with a disturbing and troubling crisis.

In his book *Pastoral Care with Children in Crisis*, Andrew Lester describes in detail numerous approaches for pastoral care and counseling with children.[21] Underlying Lester's recommendations is, first, the importance for pastors to spend more time with their young parishioners in such opportunities as Sunday school classes, Bible school, camps, and retreats. Second, the pastor should in some tangible ways demonstrate to the children that she or he knows who they are, genuinely cares about them, and has the time to talk with them. This especially can be done by engaging children in personal conversation beyond just saying "Hi" or "Hello." It is best, of course, when a pastor has laid the groundwork in church before a child begins to experience disruption in the family. When a pastoral relationship has already been established, it is more natural for the child to recognize that the pastor is a sincerely caring person who can be a genuine source of support and understanding.

Although only a few pastors may wish to develop a specialized counseling ministry with children, any pastor who makes it a point to reach out to and affirm young parishioners can have a positive pastoral influence upon their early personal and spiritual formation. To children, their pastor represents God and the church. Just the fact that such a significant representative has remembered a child's name and spoken for a few minutes with that child can help a child feel that God can be trusted when relationships at home are uncertain or frightening. The caring pastor who offers counseling to couples with children will always try to find sensitive and creative ways to show children that he or she has a genuine interest in them and their concerns.

Pastoral Counseling and Sexual Problems

Nothing may be more complex and challenging for married couples than their attempts to have a successful sexual union. Sexual feelings and responses relate deeply with every other feeling that one may have about oneself. Needs for being nurtured, pleasured, and satisfied are invariably involved in sexual interaction with one's partner. Moreover, the need to feel one is a caring spouse and a satisfying lover is very important for both husband and wife. David Mace has summarized well just how complex human sexual union can be. As he points out, both spouses must have normal and healthy sex organs. Each must have a drive to be attracted to a person of the opposite sex. Both husband and wife must find each other sexually attractive, and both need to be relatively free from negative or blocking feelings such as guilt or resentment. Additionally, Mace observes that the couple must manage successfully each individual act of intercourse so that it is satisfying to both. They must agree about how frequently, and when and where, they will come together sexually. They must keep a proper balance between their sex desires and their personal relationship with one another. And they must control procreation, by some means of contraception, in a way that is acceptable to both. Complications can arise in any or all of these areas.[22]

Furthermore, anxiety over the AIDS virus has become an increasing concern for even monogamous, heterosexual couples. AIDS has taught many people that when they have sex with someone, they are in fact having sex with everyone else their partner has ever sexually encountered, certainly with respect to AIDS and also any other sexually transmitted diseases. Therefore, it has become a wise procedure for a man and a woman anticipating their initial sexual encounter first to disclose to each other the names or backgrounds of all their former sex partners. Couples who have a trusting and faithful relationship may never be troubled about concerns that one or the other is or has become a carrier of the AIDS virus. Where such trust is not present in a marriage, the threat of possible exposure to AIDS may become a source of significant anxiety, inhibiting sexual response and enjoyment between husband and wife. Also, in some instances pastors will find themselves confronted with the ethical dilemma of whether unsuspecting spouses should be told of their partner's extramarital sexual liaisons because of the possible exposure to AIDS for both husband and wife.

The Husband's Sexual Problems

The pastor may hear concerns from either spouse about the husband having any of four possible difficulties in sexual functioning:

1. *Erectile dysfunction*, or the failure of the husband to maintain an erection for the completion of sexual intercourse, may be troubling for either one or both spouses. A man may feel that he has lost an important source of his power and his personal effectiveness as a male. His wife may also be troubled because she wants to be understanding, but she also feels frustrated by repeated unsuccessful attempts at sexual intercourse. In some instances a man may report that he has never had a satisfactory erection for intercourse at all. But more often, men with erectile dysfunction have earlier been very successful in having erections. About half the male population has experienced occasional or brief periods of erectile failure,

sometimes due to fatigue, depression, or pressing emotional concerns. Diabetes and excessive use of alcohol can also be significant causes of erectile failure. Failure to achieve a satisfactory erection can occur in men of all ages and from any socioeconomic group.

2. *Premature ejaculation* refers to a man's inability to control his orgasm, resulting in orgasm during sexual intercourse before his partner reaches her own climax. A quick or uncontrollable ejaculatory response is a common occurrence. Marital tension arises when the husband's early orgasm leads to disappointment and frustration of his wife's efforts to achieve her own sexual satisfaction. Some males are insensitive and unconcerned about their wife's disappointment. Other husbands are quite concerned that they cannot control their sexual response sufficiently in order to be a satisfying sex partner. A husband's early or uncontrolled orgasmic response can occur in any marriage and is not necessarily reflective of marital conflicts.

3. Some couples may report the husband's *inability to ejaculate* while his penis is in his wife's vagina. There can be a wide diversity in the extent of this problem, from the man who has never experienced orgasm to the husband who may occasionally not be able to reach a climax. Husbands and wives may explain that he can be successfully stimulated manually or orally, but once insertion in his wife's vagina has occurred, attempts to reach an orgasm are often unsuccessful.

Although it might be assumed that some wives are glad to have a sex partner who does not reach a premature or quick climax, a husband's recurring failure to have an orgasm can be very frustrating for his wife. Sexual intercourse in marriage includes the exchange of mutual pleasuring, and it is disappointing for partners to feel they have not pleasured their spouse as they themselves have been satisfied.

4. It is also possible that the husband's *low sex drive* may be a concern for the couple. Although men are thought to be preoccupied with sexual interests and fantasies, and although many wives feel pressured by their husbands' frequent overtures for sexual activity, it can be troubling to both spouses when the husband feels and demonstrates little or no sexual interest in his wife. The pastor should inquire in an individual session with the husband if he has another sex partner. However, if the husband denies any extramarital sexual activity, the counselor should advise the couple to consider a physical examination for the husband while also exploring marital issues and the husband's possible excessive preoccupation with business, career, or other outside interests.

The Wife's Sexual Problems

Either spouse may discuss with the pastor any of the following three areas of sexual concern for the wife:

1. In some marriages it may be a matter of concern that the wife seems to have *little or no desire for pleasure from sexual activity* with her husband. Certainly it is not unusual to hear a husband or a wife report that her sexual appetite requires less sexual activity than her husband's. Because of this difference in needs, it is easy for one spouse to conclude or imply that the other is "abnormal," "frigid," or "oversexed." All too often the word "frigid" has been used, ordinarily by frustrated husbands, to describe a wife's apparent disinterest in sexual play and intercourse. Such expressions are imprecise and pejorative, and should *never* be used by the pastor.

A few women, in fact, have never experienced erotic feelings or desired sexual activity. It is more common for some women to have enjoyed sexual experiences and orgasm but to go through phases in their marriage when their felt need for sexual satisfaction is minimal. Often the difference in sexual needs and interests between spouses can create extreme marital tension. Many women feel they must "do their duty" to satisfy their husbands, and some men seek extramarital sexual release when their sexual needs are not met by their wives.

The pastor should be careful about reaching premature conclusions about the causes for a wife's apparent lack of interest in sexual activity with her husband. Just because she may usually want sexual intercourse less often than her husband does not mean that either the wife or the husband has an abnormal appetite or need for sexual expression. Obviously, the emotional climate of the marriage can greatly affect a woman's response to her husband. Therefore, it will be essential for the couple, especially the husband, to realize that the wife's lack of interest in sexual activity is a joint challenge for them to work on together with sensitivity and caring for each other, and that it is not just *her* issue.

2. The wife *may not be having orgasms* after a previous history of orgasmic experience, or she may never have experienced an orgasm. Failure to have an orgasm can occur in women who otherwise experience sexual arousal and want to have sexual intimacy with their husbands. Despite their need for a sexual climax, they are unable to achieve an orgasm or do so only with great difficulty. Many women are unable to achieve orgasm during coitus except through simultaneous manual stimulation of their clitoris.

Psychological factors can be a strong influence in a woman's sexual response and her inability to relax and experience an orgasm. As a rule, the husband's efforts to be his wife's therapist in attempts to explain why she is inhibited will not be helpful. Work with a female counselor is probably the best way for inorgasmic women to explore the psychological conflicts that inhibit their response. Physiological factors also must be explored, such as illness, use of drugs, or hormone imbalance.

3. *Vaginismus* is a condition occurring in some women because of the involuntary spasm of the muscles at the vaginal entrance. When the woman anticipates penetration during sexual intercourse or a pelvic examination in the doctor's office, the closing of the entrance to the vagina makes the introduction of any object virtually impossible without pain and discomfort to the woman. Often women with this condition are fearful of sexual intercourse, though they may be sexually responsive and enjoy sexual play as long as it does not lead to intercourse.

Because vaginismus makes satisfactory sexual intercourse virtually impossible, the marital relationship will be under increased strain until treatment and relief are found for the condition. Vaginismus can only be diagnosed with certainty through a pelvic examination. Fortunately, the condition is highly responsive to treatment. Ordinarily, counseling is also necessary in order to help the woman resolve any associated emotional traumas.

Either husband or wife may also report experiencing pain associated with the act of sexual intercourse. The woman may describe aching, irritation, or burning in the vagina, as well as severe pain during penile thrusting. Men may have discomfort related to intercourse, the painful symptoms occurring in the several organs associated with male sexual functioning. This painful consequence of sexual intercourse in both men and women is called *dyspareunia*. Either spouse may also describe having difficulty with intercourse, or finding it impossible, because of a significant curvature of the husband's penis due to inflammation and scar tissue along the shaft of the penis. This poorly understood condition is known as *Peyronie's disease*. Referral to a urologist is recommended for examination, diagnosis, and treatment.[23]

The Pastor's Response to Sexual Issues

Most clergy are not trained or prepared to offer sex counseling. Likewise, every pastor should be very careful not to offer ill-informed or uninformed opinions about male or female sexuality. The foregoing brief discussion of the types of sex problems a couple might bring to counseling is offered only so a pastor might have an introduction to the concerns parishioners are reporting.

The most effective counseling response by the pastor to parishioners' sexual issues is listening for clarification and understanding. There is hardly any other pastoral counseling intervention in this short-term model that will be any more effective for marital sexual conflicts. In some instances, the opportunity to discuss and explore with their pastor in some detail troubling sexual concerns may help a couple to gain their own new insight and freedom to explore other options for their sexual problems.

Without being a sex therapist, a pastor can still explicitly or even implicitly reflect by attitude and concern the following positive understandings of married sexual practice.

1. Sexual pleasuring for a couple does not need to be limited to intercourse. David Mace has aptly described "the uses of noncoital sex."[24] Many couples enjoy wider expressions of their sexual love by experimenting with physical pleasuring without the expectation or demand of intercourse. Such activities that lead to orgasm without intercourse may even include the use of artificial means of stimulation such as a vibrator. Also, masturbation should be understood to be a physiologically natural act. Masturbation can have an appropriate function in a happy marriage when viewed by both partners as a natural means for relieving sexual tension when one's partner is not available.

2. Mutual respect as well as personal responsibility are important to a sexually satisfying marital relationship. Each person is a unique sexual being, and hardly any person meets the sexual stereotypes popularized in the media. Consequently, respect for and accommodation to one's partner's sexual distinctiveness is a requirement for satisfactory marital adjustment. Spouses are more likely to create an environment for meeting each other's needs when both feel a clear sense of respect and appreciation from their partner.

Likewise, sexual adjustment in marriage is more positive when both partners take responsibility for telling their spouse what they need. Operating on the assumption that one's partner will automatically know what one needs can lead to much misunderstanding and frustration in the sexual relationship.

3. Male and female bodies undergo numerous and profound changes through the aging process. These changes are quite evident to oneself and usually to one's marital partner. However, pastors should not be surprised to hear from older parishioners about their interests and needs for some kind of sexual expression and experience. Vocational retirement does not mean retirement from human sexuality.[25] The informed and accepting pastor will not convey to older couples the incredulous and naive attitude, "You still do what?"

4. In some instances a pastor will appropriately refer a couple for medical evaluation or sex therapy. A thorough medical examination is generally necessary before a sexual problem can be properly diagnosed and treated. Moreover, a physician can assess the extent to which medication, the use of alcohol or other drugs, or hormone imbalances may be factors affecting sexual response and functioning. Counselors specializing in sex therapy will typically have a consultative relationship with a physician who specializes in examinations and diagnosing for sexual dysfunctions. Ordinarily, a married couple should be referred together to a sex therapist. As a rule, if a person wants to deal individually with sexual concerns, that person should be referred to a therapist of the same gender.

A dramatically new treatment for sexual problems was introduced in March 1998, when sildenafil citrate (Viagra) was approved as the first orally active agent for the treatment of erectile dysfunction. Subsequently, research was also begun on drugs that might enhance female sexual response and pleasure. As a result of new biologically focused treatments, many sex therapists are concerned that attention will be given primarily to the use of drugs for treating sexual problems while the complex relationship conflicts that often underlie sexual difficulties are ignored. Whenever possible, pastors should refer couples with sexual problems to professionals who will include serious counseling attention to marital and relationship dynamics.[26]

5. Finally, experienced counselors know that the discussion of sexual material in a counseling session can be sexually stimulating for the counselor as well as the parishioner. Awareness of this fact can help pastors to understand their own feeling response and to exercise personal judgment about the extent to which they explore sexual matters with their counselees. Recognizing that a pastor's sexual response is to the content of the discussion and not to the counselee can help her or him to understand better what is occurring in the counseling session. To the extent a pastor feels comfortable dealing with sexual issues, the pastor's sensitive and nonjudgmental caring, within the established boundaries of the counseling relationship, can help unblock the confusion and guilt many people associate with sexual concerns.[27]

Responding to Marital Violence

There are innumerable ways in which husbands and wives can be abusive toward each other, verbally, emotionally, sexually, and physically.[28] Without diminishing the extent of pain felt from verbal and emotional abuse, attention here is given particularly to marital sexual and physical violence. Violence in a marriage is destructive of trust in such a way that it may never be regained. Violence in a marriage can tragically lead to the death of one or both spouses. Violence in a marriage typically follows a cycling pattern, and too often cannot be successfully treated or stopped.[29]

Counseling pastors can no longer be naive or uninformed about the prevalence of domestic abuse in our society. Data on marital violence have led researchers to dismaying conclusions:

> It is estimated that in one out of two marriages at least one incident of violence, probably more, will occur. In one out of five marriages the violence will be ongoing, with five or more incidents per year. At the extreme, episodes will happen monthly, weekly, or even more frequently.[30]

After surveying statistics from Canada and the United States, Nancy Nason-Clark came to this disturbing conclusion: "No matter how you define abuse, and irrespective of the manner in which you collect the data, a significant proportion of women in North America suffer physical cruelty at the hands of their husbands or partners each year."[31] No pastor should ever assume that emotional and violent abuse are not occurring in the homes of her or his parishioners. Moreover, the abusive behavior can take many forms from reckless driving, throwing and damaging possessions to rape, choking, stabbing, and beating a spouse's head against the wall or floor. Unfortunately, the church and its clergy have been supportive of social patterns that reinforce domestic and marital violence. The following observation should be a matter of concern to all pastoral counselors:

> Researchers . . . have identified religious institutions as perpetrators of wife beating because of their patriarchal attitudes. While not all denominations are patriarchal, Christian women from patriarchal churches have religious beliefs which hinder them from stopping the cycle of violence in their marital relationships.
>
> In addition to the strong influence of their religious values, Christian battered women may be hindered by an unsympathetic clergy. A minister who equates authority with control within his church may also support the right of the husband to control his wife. . . . One study . . . found that, compared to friends, relatives, lawyers, police,

women's groups, and psychologists, clergy had the lowest success rate and the highest negative influence in counseling battered women.[32]

Although husbands can be the victims of marital violence, most often wives are the ones who suffer from physical and sexual abuse.[33] It is essential for clergy to remember that it takes a great deal of courage for a woman to disclose to her pastor or to anyone that abuse is occurring in her home. Often the abusing husband does not come with his wife and is unwilling to come to subsequent meetings with the pastor. In too many instances, clergy have thus tried to counsel the wife to return to the abusive situation and to be more accommodating to her husband's needs so he will not have reason or cause to attack her again. The misguided assumption was that if the woman were sufficiently compliant to her husband's demands, marital harmony would be restored. Another misguided counseling approach has been to direct the woman to examine her own personality to see what is so wrong with herself that any man would find her hard to live with and be driven to acts of violence because of the obvious defects in her character. Certainly, the mistaken view goes, if she were less hostile or less passive or less controlling or whatever, there would be no reason for her husband to beat her up. In other words, this is "blaming the victim" for the abuser's behavior.

It is difficult to overstate how much marital violence threatens the relationship besides the obvious threat of the death of one or both spouses. Not just physical injury but even the *threat* of injury is very intimidating. And once physical abuse has occurred and the boundary against violence has been crossed, the victim lives with the constant fear—even for many years—that physical injury can happen again. Such intimidation unbalances the power for negotiation in the marriage and leaves the victim in a subordinate and often powerless position.

Additionally, if there are children in the home, they are very vulnerable emotionally and physically when violence is occurring between their parents. Not only may the children rightly fear for their own safety, but they may also try directly to intervene and stop the violence, placing them in even greater danger. Even very young children, it must be assumed, can sense that parental violence threatens the marriage and the future of the family as a unit.

Domestic violence requires pastoral intervention that may be quite different from what a minister is used to offering. Probing, insight-oriented counseling with either spouse ordinarily will not interrupt an established pattern of marital violence. Direct, active intervention is necessary, and the pastor must take a clear stand against any continuing abuse. The following guidelines (not necessarily listed in order of implementation except for no. 1) can help a counselor plan an effective pastoral strategy for intervention in marital violence.[34]

1. *Research for necessary information.* First, a pastor should make it a high priority to secure information and resources on domestic abuse, including a search on the Internet. (a) Locate a listing or directory of the human service agencies in one's area or county. Frequently, such a listing can be found through an Internet search for "information and referral" under one's state and county. The United Way can also be a source for names of agencies to which clergy can make referrals. (b) Contact local domestic abuse or domestic violence prevention programs in the area. Discuss with those sources the treatment programs they recommend for abusers. (c) Learn the state statutes for temporary restraining orders and the steps necessary for a permanent restraining order. An Internet search for statutes in the victim's state will likely find this information. (d) Learn more about domestic violence through such Internet resources as information on "The Domestic Violence Cycle" at http://incestabuse.about .com/od/domesticabuse/a/dvcycle_2.htm, and other important information at http://www.save-dv.org/stats.htm and http://endabuse.org/ resources/gethelp/. See also the General Assembly "Policy Statement on Healing Domestic Violence" at http://www.pcusa.org/oga/publications/ dancing.pdf.

2. *Always take seriously any suggestion of marital violence.* The pastor should explore very carefully any reference by either spouse to physical intimidation or abuse. Inquire when, how often, and under what circumstances such abuse has taken place. Be careful of dismissing a violent event because "it only happened one time three years ago." Also, out of fairness to both spouses, the pastor should assess exactly what has happened in order not to attribute to one spouse more abusive behavior than has actually occurred. However, it must always be remembered that if one spouse feels at all intimidated by the other, for whatever reason, such intimidation most likely plays a major disruptive role in the marriage.

3. *Take a verbal stand.* In most counseling situations, the pastor will remain neutral and not express any judgment or opinion about a counselee's behavior.[35] However, in the case of marital violence, it is essential that the pastor say clearly that there is no place for any physical abuse or violence in a marriage. Carol Adams is emphatic on this point: "Unequivocally challenge the behavior. Be ready to use clerical authority immediately to hold the abuser accountable. Accountability includes stopping the

abusive behavior and accepting the consequences of his behavior."[36] Moreover, the abusing spouse needs to be confronted with the fact that nothing the other person says can justify a physically abusive response.

4. *Inquire if there are any guns in the home.* Studies confirm that women in abusive relationships are particularly at risk when firearms are kept in the home. In one such study, the researcher made two pointed observations about women and firearms in the home:

> Among the adults studied here, the relative risk to be shot fatally (homicide) was significantly higher among women than men. This likely reflects the singular danger faced by women in abusive relationships.
>
> Keeping guns at home appears dangerous for adults regardless of age, sex, or race, but those at particularly high risk to be shot likely include persons contemplating suicide and women in abusive relationships. When patients appear suicidal or to have suffered domestic violence, the questions physicians ask should include questions about guns. Are there any guns in your home? Do you or your family members own any guns?[37]

Pastoral counselors have a similar responsibility as physicians when their counselees report domestic violence. Both of the above questions are important, because even if there are no guns in the home a person might easily gain access to a gun through a family member. If the answer to either question is yes, then the next questions should be, "What needs to be done about the guns in your home or available to you so you both feel safe and are safe?" "Should the guns be removed from your home for everyone's safety?" The individual responses by both spouses to these two questions should be taken very seriously and processed carefully by the pastor.

Some may feel that asking questions about guns in the home will only put dangerous thoughts of violence in people's minds that otherwise would not occur to them, or just scare people unnecessarily. On the contrary, asking such questions is a responsible counseling intervention that will help to alert parishioners to the increased danger they are in because there are firearms available. Included in that risk is also the possibility of a child using a gun to protect a parent. In many instances, pastors will hear one or both spouses affirm their concern about the guns in the home. Firearms in the home present a genuine life-threatening risk, and lives can be saved by asking counselees to take effective steps to prevent a tragedy from occurring in their own home.[38]

5. *Discuss a safety plan with the victim.* Often a victim will feel powerless and afraid to take any effective steps for seeking safety for oneself and for the children. The pastoral counselor should help the victim to consider all of the options available while in the abusive situation and after leaving. These recommendations are important for the victim's planning.

- Put together an "emergency kit" of things you would really need if you had to leave suddenly, such as identification, medicine, keys, and money.
- Call the National Domestic Violence Hotline at (800) 799-SAFE (799-7233) to find out about domestic violence shelters and programs in your area.
- Call the police if you are in danger.
- Remember that you are the expert about your own life. Don't let anyone talk you into doing something that's not right for you.[39]

The pastor should also secure and discuss with the victim the "Safety Plan Guidelines" offered by The National Center for Victims of Crime, accessible at http://www.ncvc.org/ncvc/main.aspx?dbName=Document Viewer&DocumentID=32452. These are thorough guidelines to help a victim consider personal safety while living with an abuser, when getting ready to leave and actually leaving, and after leaving an abusive relationship. In order to make the best decisions, it is essential that the victim be aware of the several recurring, predictable stages that culminate in violence, from the "honeymoon phase" to the "explosion and abuse phase."[40] In the course of discussing options, the pastor will also be sure that the victim has information about how to secure a temporary and a permanent restraining order.

Whatever decisions the victim makes, most often the wife, the pastor should not take any intervention steps that the victim does not know of and approve. The victim, most likely feeling without much if any effective power in the marriage, must be permitted to have the power of knowledge and consent in the counseling process.

6. *Refer the abuser for specialized treatment.* If a domestic abuse treatment program recommended by domestic abuse prevention specialists is available, the pastor should refer the abusing spouse to that program. In most cases of domestic violence, and particularly those in which a pattern of abuse can be recognized, neither promises by the abuser nor counseling by the pastor will interrupt the abusive behavior. Also participation in a treatment program does not guarantee the abusive behavior will be

stopped either. The pastor and the couple should have a frank discussion with the directors of the treatment program regarding the documented rate of success for the program.

The pastor can explain to the abuser that the treatment agency will most likely make an initial evaluation in order to determine if the abuser has a pattern of behavior that can in fact be treated in that particular program. Some persons are more willing to accept a referral from the pastor when they understand they are going first for an evaluation and not immediately into a treatment program.

7. *What to do if the abuser is accepted for treatment.* If the abuser is accepted into a domestic abuse treatment program, the necessity for the referral ends the pastoral marriage counseling. Very likely the treatment program will also include a support group and counseling for the spouse. During the course of the treatment program, the pastor will maintain regular pastoral care and contact with the couple. Following the completion of the treatment program, the couple may express interest in renewing marriage counseling with the pastor. However, the pastor should decline, declaring her or his lack of expertise in dealing with domestic violence. Adams clearly asserts that couple counseling endangers the battered spouse, and that the perpetrator can be very manipulative of the counseling process.[41] Because of the serious risks involved, and even though the abuser has completed a treatment program, the pastor should refer the couple to a professional counselor who has experience with domestic abuse.

8. *What to do if the abuser is not accepted for treatment.* Many pastors may not have specialized resources nearby to which an abusing spouse can be referred. And in some instances a treatment agency may reject a referred spouse because there is not a clear enough history of abuse for the abuser to be accepted into the program. In this case, the pastor should refer each spouse to their own counselor. It is essential for the victim to have the opportunity to examine the marriage and her or his options, including the safety of the children, in a counseling setting apart from the abuser. If, after a period of individual counseling, the victim is still persuaded it is best to reenter marriage counseling, the pastor should refer the couple to a professional counselor and not attempt to do any couple counseling.

The pastor should tell both spouses of the pastor's intention to support and encourage the victim to follow through with appropriate measures, including legal steps for protection, in order to avoid any personal injury or harm and any possible injury to the children, should any abusive threats or crises occur in the future that come to the pastor's attention. *While the pastor should be neutral in expressing pastoral care toward both spouses, the pastor cannot remain neutral about encouraging both spouses to take the necessary steps to ensure that the marital violence ends.*

When Divorce Is the Choice

Experienced pastors know that marriage counseling can very well result in the choice by one or both spouses to take steps for separation and eventual divorce. Though many divorcing couples understandably find it difficult to talk to one another without bitterness and accusations, when possible the pastor should offer to work with such couples in divorce counseling.[42]

Pastoral divorce counseling must necessarily observe similar time constraints as in pastoral marriage counseling. Typically, pastors should contract with a couple for no more than three joint divorce counseling sessions. *The divorce counseling needs to have a clear purpose of facilitating respectful communication while dealing with current and future issues arising from the dissolution of the marriage.* The purpose of divorce counseling is not to attempt to save the marriage or to review the marital conflicts and problems that led to the divorce. If a divorcing couple needs more professional attention, in the third counseling session the pastor will refer the couple to an appropriate community resource. Besides referring to individual counselors or therapists, a pastor should also make referrals to divorce support groups and programs for individuals when they are available.

The following invitation can be made to the couple:

> Pastor: I know that both of you have very reluctantly come to the conclusion that a divorce is now the only option before you. In spite of the deep and unique hurt each of you feels, and in spite of the mixed feelings you have about each other, I would like to continue working with both of you, seeing you together for another one, two or perhaps three sessions. The purpose would be to help you maintain clear and respectful communication while dealing with the important decisions you will need to make together now and in the future.
>
> Also, lawyers are usually a necessary part of the divorce process, but any communicating you can manage to do directly with each other about the details and terms of the

divorce can significantly reduce your dependence on lawyers. If after three counseling sessions here you both would like further professional counseling to help with your divorce process, I will be glad to suggest the names of counselors in the community whom I respect.

The purpose of divorce counseling or mediation is not to reestablish the marriage. Although any pastor would be thrilled to help restore a broken marital relationship, it is important that the pastor and both spouses be clear that divorce counseling is for the purpose of establishing as much reconciliation and improved communication as possible in preparation for and following a divorce.

If the pastor can be an agent for any reduction of pain, misunderstanding, bitterness, and hatred, then in most instances much will have been accomplished. A pastor may especially feel a sense of accomplishment if the divorcing couple invites the pastor, or accepts the pastor's offer, to officiate at a brief service, before God and a few witnesses, recognizing the dissolution of the marriage. Such a service can be a rich symbol for a couple that God's grace and healing are just as much with them at their parting as when they became husband and wife.[43]

Clergy should also be especially aware of divorce mediation counseling resources when they exist in the community. Mediation counselors specialize in helping divorcing couples work out legal details and arrangements for a divorce in a professional environment that controls hostility and encourages communication apart from the involvement of lawyers.[44]

One to Three More Pastoral Marriage Counseling Sessions

If a pastor recontracts with a couple for more pastoral marriage counseling sessions, the sessions should be scheduled on a one-at-a-time basis without the automatic assumption that the couple will use all three follow-up counseling sessions. Moreover, it is essential that the couple be sufficiently stable and conflict-free that no more than one to three supportive sessions with their pastor will be necessary.

The follow-up sessions will be most helpful and productive for the couple if the pastor directs them in a process for setting specific goals and objectives to be accomplished before the next counseling session. In other words, this is action-focused counseling, not just unstructured conversation. The most progress for the couple will occur between counseling sessions as they reinforce new relationship behaviors and focus their efforts on the growth tasks they jointly decide need their attention.

Appendix E is the form Planning for Follow-up Pastoral Marriage Counseling (PFPMC). If the decision is made by the couple and the pastor in the final counseling session for them to recontract for a follow-up marriage counseling session, the pastor will immediately use the PFPMC form to prepare the couple for their first follow-up session. The pastor will give the couple a copy of the form and will keep another copy. The pastor and the couple will work through the form, discussing with each other the questions as the couple prepares their responses. The couple will then take their copy of the form home with them, and the pastor will retain his or her copy for reference in the next counseling session.

The purpose of the PFPMC form is to enable the couple to determine the best areas for them to take specific, concrete action toward the improvement of their marriage. The form will then provide the basis for the first follow-up pastoral marriage counseling session. *Using the PFPMC will give intentional and productive direction to the counseling process, helping the couple to make the best use of the opportunity to do more counseling with their pastor.*

The first follow-up counseling session may be scheduled within one to three weeks. All of the follow-up marriage counseling sessions will proceed along the same outline observed in the third couple counseling session described in chapter 4 (see summary on page 109). The counseling process has six elements: (1) check out present relating; (2) define the purpose of the session; (3) evaluate the growth task(s) using the PFPMC; (4) assess progress; (5) make recommendations; and (6) affirm the couple, give the couple the pastor's copy of the PFPMC, and close with prayer.

A couple may decide that one follow-up marriage counseling session with their pastor is all that they need, or they and their pastor may schedule the second follow-up session another one to three weeks in the future. In that case, another PFPMC form should be reviewed and completed, again with a copy for the couple and a copy for the pastor. The couple will once again take the form home with them with the new specific marriage growth task(s) to be accomplished. If the third follow-up counseling session is scheduled, the same procedure should be observed with the PFPMC, with the same six process elements observed as were followed in the first two follow-up couple counseling sessions. Of course, referring the couple to a professional marriage counselor in the community may be appropriate after any one of the follow-up counseling sessions.

Conclusion: A Compelling
Responsibility and Call

It is ironic that marriage holds out the possibility for the greatest, most fulfilling joy and the worst of emotional pain. Marriage unquestionably is, as David and Vera Mace have described it, a relationship of "terrifying closeness."[45] And the children of the generations that follow most marriages are profoundly influenced by the marital decisions and conflicts of their parents, their grandparents, and even their great-grandparents. Because so much is at stake in modern marriages, the purpose of this book has been to outline for pastors a sound counseling plan so they can confidently intervene in a professionally responsible manner in the troubled marriages of their parishioners.

The challenge to the church in its heritage and tradition of the pastoral care of souls is to be present wherever alienation disrupts human lives and relationships. More than forty years ago Charles Stewart began his book on the minister as marriage counselor with the observation that "the days of the 'lick-and-a-promise' session with a couple to be married and of the solemn prayer and little else over the quarreling couple are rapidly drawing to a close."[46] Marriage counseling today is a compelling responsibility and a call that must be taken seriously by every pastor. The plan for this pastoral short-term marriage counseling model, grounded in the certain presence of God and the empowering promise of the miracle of dialogue, goes far beyond a solemn prayer over a quarreling couple to bring a promising and hopeful pastoral intervention to troubled parishioners. Now an increasing number of marriages can find renewed love, stability, and growth, because pastors faithfully and confidently can say to their parishioners, "I have a plan," and join with them in the exciting process of God's healing for broken relationships.

Appendix A

Covenant for
Pastoral Marriage Counseling

It is essential for a couple to understand clearly what pastoral marriage counseling *is* and what it *is not*. *The purpose of pastoral marriage counseling is to be an opportunity for a couple to work together with their pastor in order to understand and resolve conflict, and to enhance and enrich their marriage.*

1. Marriage counseling is a *process* for learning more about oneself, one's partner, and the marital relationship.
2. The pastor does not give advice or answers. The goal of the counseling is for both spouses individually to make their own best, informed decisions for themselves, for their marriage, and for their family.
3. Pastoral marriage counseling is a very hopeful process, but there is no guarantee about the final outcome.
4. Each person can change only herself or himself and not the other person.
5. Nothing is gained by using the counseling for talking about all the ways one's partner behaves in an "outrageous" manner.
6. Counseling sessions are not to be used for fighting or attacking each other.
7. It is not the pastor's job to be a judge taking sides and deciding who is right and wrong.
8. It is not the purpose of marriage counseling for one spouse to bring the other so the other will get help or get counseling.
9. Likewise, it is also not the purpose of marriage counseling for the pastor to make an assessment in order to determine which spouse is "sick" or "sicker" than the other.

10. *The focus of pastoral marriage counseling is on the relationship and what both spouses want to change about themselves and their contribution to the marriage.*

Pastoral marriage counseling is for a husband and wife who want:

1. To work *together* to find better ways for their marriage to be more satisfying for each of them.
2. To find ways to communicate important feelings in a manner that is *respectful* of each other.

The plan for pastoral marriage counseling is for the couple to meet initially together with their pastor. Then the pastor sees each person separately once or twice before seeing them together as a couple for two more sessions. A questionnaire is given to each person to be completed for the pastor to read before the first individual session. At the final session, the couple and the pastor will evaluate the couple's progress and decide upon one of three options: (1) termination of marriage counseling, (2) referral to another professional counseling resource, or (3) one to three follow-up marriage counseling sessions with the pastor. An early referral to another professional counselor and termination of this counseling process can be made at any time if necessary. All counseling sessions will be fifty to sixty minutes in length.

This covenant for marriage counseling assumes that both spouses are committed solely to their marriage. If either spouse is presently involved in an extramarital romantic and/or sexual relationship, no progress can be made on the marriage, nor will marriage counseling be useful.

We understand the purpose and procedures for pastoral marriage counseling, and covenant with God, with each other, and with our pastor to work together in order to find better ways to strengthen our marital relationship.

_____ _____

Date: _____

Pastoral Marriage Counseling Questionnaire*

The purpose of this questionnaire is to help you reflect on issues and dynamics related to your marriage. This information will also assist your pastor to explore with you the various resources and options you and your partner have for resolving conflicts and strengthening your relationship. Though it takes time to complete these questions, many persons find that this questionnaire helps them to clarify their feelings and understandings.

Do not share your written responses with your partner. Your questionnaire will be returned to you after the counseling sessions have come to an end.

Name _____ Age_____

Occupation _____

Current address _____

Home telephone number _____ Work telephone number_____

Spouse's name _____ Age_____

Spouse's occupation _____

Spouse's current address_____

Spouse's home telephone _____ Spouse's work telephone _____

---

*Additional space for writing should be added when the questionnaire is reproduced.

Courtship and Marriage

1. How did you and your spouse first meet?

2. What were your reasons for marrying your spouse?

3. What was your honeymoon like, and what were your feelings about it?

4. Do you have any children? If yes, what are their names, ages, and grades in school?

5. Do you have any children who live outside the home? If so, where?

6. If any children are no longer living, when and how did they die?

7. Have you or your spouse been married before? If so, when, how, and why did that/those marriage(s) end?

8. Is the amount of your time, or your spouse's time, spent on the computer and the Internet—or subjects of particular interest on the computer/Internet—a matter of concern for either of you? If yes, please explain.

9. Is the amount of time either of you spends away from home a matter of concern for either of you? If yes, please explain.

10. Do the current problems in your marriage include any of the following?
    Circle those that apply.
    a. Lack of communication
    b. Sexual or physical abuse
    c. Infidelity
    d. In-law overinvolvement
    e. Finances
    f. Problems relating to children
    g. Work-related problems
    h. Alcohol or chemical abuse
    i. Sexual problems
    j. Unfulfilled emotional needs
    k. Lack of spiritual growth
    l. Premenstrual syndrome (PMS)
    m. Other (specify)
    On a blank sheet please elaborate on each of the items you circled.

11. For your marriage to be more satisfying, what do you think your spouse needs to change?

12. For your marriage to be more satisfying, what do you think you need to change within or about yourself?

13. What are you willing to change?

Family of Origin

14. Father's name _____

    Age if living _____ Deceased? Date _____ Age_____

    Occupation_____

15. Mother's name _____

    Age if living _____ Deceased? Date _____ Age_____

    Occupation_____

16. Do you have any brothers or sisters, living or dead? If so, list their names and ages, beginning with the oldest. Place yourself in the list.

17. Describe your relationship with your father until you left home, and currently.

18. Describe your relationship with your mother until you left home, and currently.

19. In a few sentences state how your family of origin was unique or different from other families.

20. Upon reflection, what do you think your role was in your family of origin? That is, what did you make possible for your family by your presence and your behavior?

21. Is there any history of alcohol or chemical abuse in your present or original family? If yes, please describe.

22. Is there any history of sexual or physical abuse in your present or original family? If yes, please describe.

Personal Information

23. Do you take any medication? If yes, please give name(s) and dosage.

    Prescribed by _____ When_____

    For what condition? _____

Any side effects?_____

24. Have you ever had any serious illness(es) or been hospitalized? If yes, please describe and give dates.

25. Do you or your spouse have any health or physical limitations, handicaps, or impairments that affect your relationship? If yes, please explain.

26. How much regular coffee, tea, cola, or other caffeine-containing beverages do you drink?

27. What is your current appetite and eating pattern?

28. Describe any gain or loss in your weight in the last two years.

29. Describe your sleep pattern—when you sleep and any difficulties you associate with sleeping.

30. Is your religion or faith a positive or a negative resource for you and for your marriage? Please explain.

31. Please describe any work-related concerns or conflicts you or your spouse are currently experiencing.

32. Have you ever had any previous professional counseling? If yes, give dates, the purpose of the counseling, and the name of the counselor or agency.

33. Have you or your spouse ever tried to commit suicide? If yes, give the date(s) and briefly describe the circumstances.

34. Please describe briefly and give the dates for the times in your life when you have had any thoughts, feelings, or experiences that were unusual or disturbing for you.

35. Describe yourself as you understand your personality.

Possible Critical Issues in the First Session

1. *Extramarital affairs*
   a. Reference by either spouse to a past affair needs to be assessed in subsequent sessions for how much stress and pain is currently in the marriage because of it.
   b. A current affair acknowledged by either spouse precludes any effective work by the couple in marriage counseling. Ordinarily, refer each spouse immediately to separate professional counselors. If the spouses think they still want marriage counseling in spite of the ongoing affair, refer them immediately to a professional marriage therapist.

2. *Alcohol or chemical abuse*
   a. State that you are not an alcohol or chemical dependency evaluator. Also say that regardless of how much or how little a spouse may use alcohol or chemicals, if the other spouse sees it as an issue, then it is an important issue in the marriage.
   b. Say, "If one of you is abusing or dependent on alcohol or chemicals, then marriage counseling will accomplish little if anything until that person receives treatment."
   c. In the initial session give both spouses information or brochures for local Alcoholics Anonymous/Al-Anon meetings and area treatment programs, encouraging both spouses to seriously consider those programs.
   d. Having flagged the alcohol or chemical abuse as a major issue, you may continue with the marriage counseling plan if that is the couple's desire and choice.

3. *Domestic violence*
   a. Any reported past abuse in the relationship, no matter how long ago it occurred, must not be discounted but affirmed as a potentially troubling present factor in the marriage.
   b. Any current abuse must stop. Say, "The physical/sexual abuse must stop immediately. It is destructive to your marriage and makes it impossible for trust to be regained." No excuse is accepted that seeks to justify the abuse. This stand is taken by the pastor at the risk of alienating the abuser.
   c. If there are any children, ask if they are safe or if they have been abused.
   d. Inquire if there are any guns in the home or elsewhere available to either spouse. If guns are present, ask what needs to be done to ensure the safety of everyone in the family, including removing the guns from the home.
   e. Give both spouses literature or brochures for domestic abuse telephone hotlines and treatment programs. Refer the abuser immediately to a domestic abuse treatment program. Do not proceed any further with the marriage counseling.
   f. Tell the couple that you will continue your pastoral care and contact with each of them and that you will want to know what comes of the abuser's meeting with the abuse treatment resource.
   g. Make a special point to follow up very soon with the victim to help with the consideration of all options and the formulation of a safety plan that includes getting legal and police intervention, if necessary, and leaving the home and possibly the relationship.

4. *Obvious mental health issues*
   a. It is routine for spouses in conflict to maintain that the other is somehow "crazy" or "sick." The behavior referred to by either spouse most often will be typical of the countless ways conflicted spouses go about making each other miserable.
   b. A serious mental health issue in one or the other spouse, on the other hand, may very well be recognized and affirmed by both spouses. They may acknowledge that the mental health distress is dominating their relationship and seriously contributing to increased conflict or tension in the marriage.
   c. The more accepting both spouses are of the dominant and distracting role of the mental health issue, the more likely they are to be

open to an immediate referral to a mental health professional or family physician.

d. In most instances, it is best to postpone pastoral marriage counseling until the dominating mental health issue has been addressed.

e. If a couple is not prepared for an immediate referral and wants to continue with the marriage counseling plan, the counseling process may prepare the couple for a referral at the final session to a mental health professional or family physician.

5. *Compulsive gambling or sexual addiction reported to be a disturbing factor in the marriage*

a. Clarify and understand the information that is reported.

b. Do not adopt or use the labels "compulsive gambling" or "sexual addiction."

c. Assure the couple that you will explore this issue carefully with each of them in the individual sessions.

6. *One or both spouses not wanting to proceed with the marriage counseling plan*

a. Respect any reluctance to participate in further marriage counseling. Unmotivated participation on the part of one spouse will most likely raise unwarranted hope in the other spouse, only leading later to greater disappointment over the failure of the counseling.

b. Explore if either spouse wants to be referred to a professional counselor for personal therapy and support.

c. Assure the couple of your intention to continue to be a pastor to them and their children without siding with either spouse. Also, assure both spouses that you will pray for them and for their family and children.

d. Extend an open-ended invitation for the pastoral marriage counseling plan if both spouses decide later they want to work together on their marriage.

7. *One or both spouses not having the education or verbal skills to complete the questionnaire*

a. Explain that the questions on the questionnaire are important in helping both spouses better understand the troubling issues in their marriage.

b. Offer a choice among three options.

(1) The spouses can take their questionnaires home and read them.

They can write one or a couple words in response to each question, and then they can discuss each response with you in one or two individual sessions.

(2) The spouses can take their questionnaires home and read them without providing any written responses. They can then discuss the questionnaire a question at a time with you in one or two individual sessions.

(3) If a spouse cannot read at all, assure that person that he or she can discuss the questionnaire with you one question at a time in one or two individual sessions.

Appendix D

Managing Critical Issues

1. Always adhere closely to the guidelines and boundaries of the short-term counseling plan.

2. Use a consulting resource of clergy peers and/or a professional counseling therapist.

3. Note appendix C procedures.

4. *Mandated reporting.* Mandated reporting for clergy to report the abuse of children or vulnerable adults may require difficult pastoral decisions. However, the safety of the person being abused must be the first pastoral consideration. Furthermore, do not hesitate to inquire about possible abuse even though you know you may be in a position of having to make a report to authorities.

5. *Domestic violence.* The safety of the person being abused and the children in the home is the primary concern for the pastor. Earlier incidents of abuse may still be intimidating to the victim. The pastor takes a stand and confronts the physical and sexual abuse, saying how destructive it is to the marriage and that the abuse must stop. The pastor also asks if the children are safe or if they have been abused. Inquire about the presence of any guns in the home and their removal for everyone's safety. The pastoral marriage counseling ends, and the abuser is referred to a professional resource or agency that treats domestic abuse. Even for past abusive incidents, the couple needs the assistance of a specialist in domestic abuse to help the couple assess the current risk and threat of abuse to the marriage. In individual sessions with the victim, the pastor will help the victim devise a safety plan for leaving the abuser, leaving the home, very possibly leaving the relationship, and seeking a restraining order. Because couple counseling can endanger an abused spouse, the pastor does not do any

future marriage counseling with the couple, but refers to a professional counselor if the couple requests counseling again.

6. *Extramarital affairs.* Marriage counseling will not be effective while one of the spouses is involved in a romantic or sexual extramarital relationship. Nor can marriage counseling be used by a spouse to decide which relationship to choose. If a pastor learns that one of the spouses is involved in a current affair, that spouse should be referred for individual counseling. The other spouse should also be referred to another counselor for supportive counseling. Many couples have survived an extramarital affair, but the rebuilding of the marriage and the regaining of trust requires the wholehearted recommitment of both spouses to the marriage.

7. *Alcohol or chemical abuse.* If alcohol or chemical use appears to contribute to the tension in the marriage, the pastor may rightly suspect that there is an addiction. The pastor should explain to the couple that if there is an addiction, progress with marriage counseling will be highly unlikely. The abusing spouse should be referred to a treatment center or program for evaluation, while the other spouse is referred to Al-Anon, or other supportive resource for the abuse of other chemicals. Alcoholics Anonymous may also be an effective resource for the abusing spouse. Marriage counseling can be promising when spouses convincingly demonstrate that their use of alcohol or other chemicals does not contribute to marital conflict or problems.

8. *Compulsive gambling or sexual addiction.* Do not adopt the diagnosis or label offered by one spouse that describes the other as addicted to gambling or sex. Such a diagnosis should properly be made by a professional specializing in the treatment of gambling or sexual addiction. If there is evidence of repeated or apparently uncontrolled behavior that has a severe or destructive impact on the marriage, a referral for evaluation and treatment is in order and needs to take precedence over the pastoral marriage counseling. However, before making that referral, first consult with a professional counselor to ensure that a referral is appropriate. The other spouse should be referred to a support resource for family members of persons with compulsive gambling or uncontrolled sexual behavior.

9. *Divorce is the outcome.* Look for the opportunity to offer brief divorce counseling to the separating couple. The counseling will go no more than three sessions, and the focus will be on improved communication and the reduction of tension, *not* on recovery of the marriage. Likewise, effective divorce counseling may also facilitate some expression of forgiveness for past wrongs and hurts felt by each of the spouses. The pastor should also

consider with the couple whether a brief service might be helpful and appropriate, officiated by the pastor, to acknowledge before God and perhaps some appropriate witnesses their broken covenant relationship and to release each other from their vows.[1] You tell the couple that you will continue your pastoral care and concern for each of them beyond the divorce process.

Planning for Follow-up Pastoral Marriage Counseling

The pastor and the couple will complete this form together, the couple writing on one copy and the pastor on a second copy. The best progress on a marriage can ordinarily be accomplished when a couple directs their attention to the completion of specific tasks where they feel growth is needed in the marriage. The following goal(s) and growth tasks(s) will be discussed at the next marriage counseling session on _____.

1. Name general areas or goals for marital growth. These goals will *not* be specific. Examples are: developing better communication, spending more quality time together, and having more fun together. One to three goals will be sufficient.

a. _____

b. _____

c. _____

2. Identify at least one specific objective or growth task to be accomplished for each goal. An example of a specific growth task for better communication would be, "Sunday, Monday, and Wednesday evenings from 7:30 until 8:00, we will turn off the TV and discuss with each other the events of the day, and review commitments on the family calendar for the next four days." One to six growth tasks will be enough.

a. _____

b. _____

c. _____

d. _____

e. _____

f. _____

_____   _____
spouses' signatures

Date: _____

Pastoral Marriage Counseling Action Checklist

1. Make copies of the Covenant for Pastoral Marriage Counseling and the Pastoral Marriage Counseling Questionnaire.
2. Make copies of process summaries in chapters 2–4, and appendixes C, D, E, and F.
3. Set up three chairs in the office, with a clock and tissue box available.
4. Call the appropriate state or local authorities to learn the mandated expectations for clergy to report abuse situations.
5. Inquire from an appropriate legal source information about temporary and permanent restraining orders as they apply to domestic violence.
6. Through the Internet, the United Way, or a local social services office, locate the information and referral directory of human services agencies in your area. See also http://211.org/about.html.
7. Research the availability in your community of:
   a. respected professionals doing individual, marriage, and family therapy;
   b. domestic abuse treatment;
   c. alcohol or chemical abuse treatment;
   d. compulsive gambling and sexual addiction treatment; and
   e. sex therapy.
8. Find and secure information from:

   - American Bar Association—Commission on Domestic Violence
     www.abanet.org/domviol/home.html

- Family Violence Prevention Fund
  www.fvpf.org
- National Coalition Against Domestic Violence
  www.ncadv.org
- National Domestic Violence Hotline
  1-800-799-7233
  1-800-787-3224 TTY
  www.ndvh.org
- National Network to End Domestic Violence
  www.nnedv.org
- Office on Violence Against Women
  www.ojp.usdoj.gov/vawo

9. Talk personally with all potential referral resources, and inquire how services are offered and fees charged. Secure business cards and brochures for distribution to counselees. Not all Alcoholics Anonymous, Al-Anon, and Adult Children of Alcoholics groups are the same. Learn details about specific groups to which you may wish to make referrals.
10. Take a leadership role in forming a peer counseling case review group.
11. Find a professional counselor, therapist, or physician with whom to discuss counseling cases.
12. Review with the adult Christian education committee the scheduling of marriage enrichment and support programs on Sundays and at weekday educational times.
13. Research and become acquainted with such marriage enrichment resources as:

- The Association for Couples in Marriage Enrichment
  http://www.bettermarriages.org
- The Coalition for Marriage, Family, and Couples Education
  http://www.smartmarriages.com
- Couple Communication Program/Interpersonal Communication Programs, Inc.
  http://www.couplecommunication.com
- Marriage Enrichment
  http://www.marriageenrichment.org
- National Marriage Encounter
  http://www.marriage-encounter.org

14. Within your own church or group of community churches organize a divorce support ministry with regular program meetings and support groups.
15. Review the notes and bibliography in this book for possible helpful information.

Notes

Full facts of publication for books referred to only by author and title may be found in the bibliography.

Chapter 1: I Have a Plan

1. "The results indicate that the percentage of adults under 45 years old who may ever marry may be around the 90-percent level, while the percentage of first marriages ending in divorce may be as high as 50 percent." This is one of the conclusions from a U.S. Census Bureau report on marriage and divorce. See Rose M. Kreider and Jason M. Fields, *Number, Timing, and Duration of Marriages and Divorces: Fall 1996*, 19. Current Population Reports, P70-80. (Washington, DC: U.S. Census Bureau, 2001). This report is available online at http://www.census.gov/prod/2002pubs/p70-80.pdf.

2. One pastor told me that the area judicatory supervising his ministry now requires all of its parish clergy to engage only in short-term pastoral counseling. Because of growing concern about legal and insurance liabilities, this requirement could become the policy of more church judicatories across many denominations.

3. See Neil S. Jacobson and Alan S. Gurman, eds., *Clinical Handbook of Couple Therapy* (New York: Guilford Press, 1995).

4. See "Married-Couple and Unmarried-Partner Households: 2000," Census 2000 Special Reports, U.S. Census Bureau, February 2003, 1, available online at http://www.census.gov/prod/2003pubs/censr-5.pdf.

5. See "The Care of 'Living Together' Couples" (an interview with Wayne E. Oates), *Family Ministry: Empowering Through Faith* 12, no. 3 (Fall 1998): 57–60.

6. Garland and Garland, *Beyond Companionship*, 51.

7. Culbertson, *Caring for God's People*, 154.

8. A popular example is Hendrix, *Getting the Love You Want*. Note Hendrix's description of the "unconscious marriage" and the "conscious marriage," in parts 1 and 2.

9. Tillich, *Systematic Theology*, 1:174–86.

10. Ibid., 282.

11. Ibid., 181.

12. See Sager, *Marriage Contracts and Couple Therapy*.

160   *Notes*

13. Tillich, *Systematic Theology*, 1:185.
14. Ibid., 184.
15. See Denise Previti and Paul R. Amato, "Why Stay Married? Rewards, Barriers, and Marital Stability," *Journal of Marriage and Family* 65, no. 3 (August 2003): 561–73. This article reports on a national, seventeen-year longitudinal study of marital instability. The researchers found evidence for eleven positive reinforcing categories for marriage: love, respect, trust, communication, shared past, friendship, happiness, compatibility, emotional security, commitment to the partner, and sex. These categories are similar to the ten "vital signs" I have found in twenty-nine years of marriage counseling. Judith S. Wallerstein and Sandra Blakeslee have contended that a good marriage is built on a series of nine life changes or sequential psychological tasks. While there is some overlapping, the ten "vital signs" will help couples deal successfully with the nine psychological tasks. See Wallerstein and Blakeslee, *Good Marriage*, 27–28, 331–32.
16. Clinebell and Clinebell, *Intimate Marriage*, 36.
17. *Merriam-Webster's Collegiate Dictionary*, 11th ed. (Springfield, MA: Merriam-Webster, 2003), 567.
18. This topic is developed more fully in Charles L. Rassieur, "Dialogue: The Continuing Imperative," in *Festschrift in Honor of Charles Speel*, ed. Thomas J. Sienkewicz and James E. Betts (Monmouth, IL: Monmouth College, 1996), 196–212. This essay is available online at http://department.monm.edu/classics/Speel_Festschrift/rassieur.htm.
19. Buber, *I and Thou*, 10, (*I-Thou*) inserted in view of Buber's statements, "The primary word *I-Thou* can only be spoken with the whole being," 3 and 11.
20. Buber, *Between Man and Man*, 97.
21. Ibid., 30.
22. Howe, *Miracle of Dialogue*, 8.
23. Lester, *Hope in Pastoral Care and Counseling*, 85, 89.
24. Howe, *Miracle of Dialogue*, 83.
25. Ibid., 69–83. The list that follows is a summary of Howe's characteristics of a dialogical person.
26. Ibid., 78.
27. Ibid., 83.
28. Oates, *Christian Pastor*, 79.

Chapter 2: Putting the Plan into Action

1. Stone, *Brief Pastoral Counseling*, 7.
2. Stone, *Strategies for Brief Pastoral Counseling*, 199. See discussion, 197–99. See also the following discussions of short-term counseling in the parish (although these do not offer a model for short-term pastoral marriage counseling): Capps, *Giving Counsel*, 194–200, 205–10 (see also Capps's outline of John C. Wynn's ninety-minute couple counseling process, 125–26); Brian H. Childs, *Short-Term Pastoral Counseling: A Guide* (Nashville: Abingdon Press, 1990); Culbertson, *Caring for God's People*, 260–62. H. Clinebell discusses short-term parish marriage counseling of four to five sessions in *Basic Types of Pastoral Care and Counseling*, 262, as well as in *Basic Types of Pastoral Counseling*, 115–16. The reader is also directed to Carroll A. Wise, *Pastoral Counseling: Its Theory and Practice* (New York: Harper & Brothers, 1951, 187–88), for a statement of the earlier view that it is better to see spouses individually for marriage counseling until each has achieved his or her own individual understanding, acceptance, and growth.

3. See David K. Switzer's discussion of the symbolic power of the minister as a counselor in *Minister as Crisis Counselor*, 15–16. See also Oates, *Christian Pastor*, 65–95 (chap. 2, "The Symbolic Power of the Pastor").

4. Dittes, *Pastoral Counseling*, 5.

5. Clinebell, *Basic Types of Pastoral Care and Counseling*, 286–90.

6. The CPMC is slightly revised from Guidelines for Marital Therapy (GMT), which I created and used with every couple I saw in the last eight years of my private practice as a counseling psychologist. I always introduced the GMT to the couple in the first counseling session. There was virtually total acceptance and appreciation of the form by every couple. In nearly every instance couples were relieved to understand that the counseling process would be fair and without manipulation of either spouse. Most notable was how couples moved beyond their instinctive adversarial posture to a hopeful attitude by the end of the initial session. Of course, throughout the subsequent counseling process occasions would arise when I had to remind the couples of the counseling guidelines they had agreed to observe.

7. See note 28 in chapter 5, for a definition of domestic violence.

8. Stewart, *Minister as Marriage Counselor* (1970) 81.

Chapter 3: The Plan for Meeting with Each Spouse

1. Brian W. Grant, *Reclaiming the Dream: Marriage Counseling in the Parish Context* (Nashville: Abingdon Press, 1986), 54–57.

2. Ibid., 62.

3. These data are from a January 23, 2003, speech, slide 5, by Sybil K. Goldman, senior advisor on children for the Substance Abuse and Mental Health Services Administration, an agency of the U.S. Department of Health and Human Services. This speech is available online at http://www.mentalhealth.org/newsroom/speeches/keynote.asp.

4. "Not only is there a wide array of sexual 'chat rooms,' erotic and pornographic websites, and special interest groups, there is also a virtual treasure-house of sexual paraphernalia and erotica for individuals of every sexual predilection. Increasingly, clinicians are being asked to treat individuals and couples for whom the diversions of cyberspace have proven disruptive or that have negatively impacted their own lives or that of their children and/or partners." Sandra R. Leiblum and Raymond C. Rosen, "Introduction: Sex Therapy in the Age of Viagra," in *Principles and Practice of Sex Therapy*, 3rd ed., edited by Sandra R. Leiblum and Raymond C. Rosen (New York: Guilford Press, 2000), 9.

5. See Wegscheider-Cruse, *Another Chance*, 89–149.

6. See Jay and Jay, *Love First*.

7. Masters, Johnson, and Kolodny, *Masters and Johnson on Sex and Human Loving*, 233–34.

8. *Diagnostic and Statistical Manual of Mental Disorders* (DSM-IV), 4th ed. (Washington, DC: American Psychiatric Association, 1994), 715–18. Also see Aetna InteliHealth on Premenstrual Syndrome (PMS) for medical information reviewed by the faculty of the Harvard Medical School. This is available online at http://www.intelihealth.com/IH/ihtIH/EMIHC000/9339/23664.html.

9. See Woititz, *Adult Children of Alcoholics*, and Resources for Adult Children of Alcoholics at http://www.drjan.com.

10. I always used these six questions in my counseling practice when meeting with individual marriage partners.

11. Neil S. Jacobson and Andrew Christensen, *Integrative Couple Therapy: Promoting Acceptance and Change* (New York: W. W. Norton & Co., 1996), 156.
12. See the following: Indiana University, "What Are Addictive Behaviors?" http://www.indiana.edu/~engs/hints/addictiveb.html; Minnesota Institute of Public Health, "Gambling: Choices and Guidelines," http://www.naspl.org/choices.html; Gamblers Anonymous home page: http://www.gamblersanonymous.org; Carnes, *Out of the Shadows*; Carnes, *Contrary to Love*; and Carnes's resources for sex addiction and recovery at http://www.sexhelp.com/sa_q_and_a.cfm. See also Carnes et al., *In the Shadows of the Net*.

Chapter 4: The Plan for the Final Two Sessions

1. Chemical abuse is more technically identified as a *substance* referring to a drug of abuse, a medication, or a toxin in the *Diagnostic and Statistical Manual of Mental Disorders* (DSM-IV), 4th ed. (Washington, DC: American Psychiatric Association, 1994), 175–272. See resources available online to aid a pastor's response to alcohol or chemical abuse at the following Web sites:
   Adult Children of Alcoholics http://www.adultchildren.org)
   Alcoholics Anonymous (http://www.alcoholics-anonymous.org)
   Al-Anon/Alateen (http://www.al-anon.alateen.org)
   Cocaine Anonymous (http://www.ca.org)
   Narcotics Anonymous (http://www.na.org)
   Drug and alcohol abuse treatment programs can be found at http://findtreatment.samhsa.gov/facilitylocatordoc.htm.
2. See note 28 in chapter 5 for a fuller description of domestic violence.
3. Stone, *Strategies for Brief Pastoral Counseling*, 102.

Chapter 5: The Plan for Counseling Challenges

1. William R. Miller and Kathleen A. Jackson, *Practical Psychology for Pastors* (Englewood Cliffs, NJ: Prentice-Hall, 1985), 26.
2. Further information about the AAPC and resources in one's area may be obtained through the national office of the AAPC at 9504A Lee Highway, Fairfax, VA 22031-2303. The AAPC phone number is (703) 385-6967. The AAPC Web site is at http://www.aapc.org, and the e-mail address is info@aapc.org.
3. The address of the national office of the AAMFT is 112 South Alfred Street, Alexandria, VA 22314-3061. The AAMFT phone number is (703) 838-9808. The AAMFT Web site is at http://www.aamft.org, and the e-mail address is central@aamft.org.
4. For example, Internet references to new state statutes making clergy mandated reporters in Massachusetts and Colorado can be found at http://www.macucc.org/leadership/confidential.htm, and http://www.rothgerber.com/newslettersarticles/ff016.asp.
5. Tournier, *To Understand Each Other*, 38.
6. Capps, *Giving Counsel*, 247.
7. Augsburger, *Pastoral Counseling across Cultures*, 30.
8. Carol Gilligan, *In a Different Voice: Psychological Theory and Women's Development* (Cambridge, MA: Harvard University Press, 1982), 173.
9. Augsburger, *Pastoral Counseling across Cultures*, 18.
10. See the U.S. Census Bureau's 2004 report, "U.S. Interim Projections by Age, Sex, Race, and Hispanic Origin," table 1A, which is available online at http://www.census.gov/ipc/www/usinterimproj.

11. To give a personal example, I was grateful when a gay pastor explained to me that the way gay couples view friends is very different from a heterosexual point of view. The pastor explained that friends for heterosexual people are not as vital as they are for gay persons, because friends in the gay culture are, for example, necessary for a sense of caring family support. Many gay people have been rejected by their families and too often by their original friends. So their present friends fill an essential need for acceptance, understanding, and emotional support that heterosexual people usually find in their own families.

12. Clinebell, *Basic Types of Pastoral Care and Counseling*, 101. See also Culbertson, *Caring for God's People*, 274–75.

13. Wiest and Smith, *Ethics in Ministry*, 186.

14. See Rassieur, *Problem Clergymen Don't Talk About*. In this book I discuss the male pastor's sexual response in the counseling session. See also Rutter, *Sex in the Forbidden Zone*; and Lebacqz and Barton, *Sex in the Parish*.

15. Professional ethics for clergy have been reexamined recently by some who assert that a strictly professional ethics model does not fit parish ministry. See Lebacqz and Driskill, *Ethics and Spiritual Care*, 37–55. The writers acknowledge that there is more to clergy ethics than setting appropriate boundaries, but they emphasize that "protections against abuse must be structured into any clergy ethics, if those ethics are to be credible" (55). See also Marie M. Fortune, "The Joy of Boundaries," in Ragsdale, *Boundary Wars*.

16. James L. Peterson and Nicholas Zill, "Marital Disruption, Parent-Child Relationships, and Behavior Problems in Children," *Journal of Marriage and the Family* (May 1986): 295.

17. See Office of the General Assembly, 21. "Turn Mourning into Dancing!" The "Policy Statement" references "American Psychological Association, Violence and the Family: Report of the American Psychological Association Presidential Task Force on Violence and the Family" (1996), 80.

18. Lester, *Pastoral Care with Children in Crisis*, 49.

19. Sanford L. Braver and Jeffrey T. Cookston, "Controversies, Clarifications, and Consequences of Divorce's Legacy: Introduction to the Special Collection," *Family Relations Interdisciplinary Journal of Applied Family Studie*s 52, no. 4 (October 2003): 314. All the articles in this edition of the journal pertain to the legacy of divorce.

20. See Wallerstein et al., *Unexpected Legacy of Divorce*. Note especially the concluding advice to parents in unhappy marriages on pp. 307–9.

21. See chapter 4 of Lester, *Pastoral Care with Children in Crisis* ("Some Basic Principles of Pastoral Care to Children"). See also Benjamin T. Griffin, "Children Whose Parents Are Divorcing," in Lester, *When Children Suffer*, 69–81.

22. David Mace, *Sexual Difficulties in Marriage* (Philadelphia: Fortress Press, 1972), 11–12.

23. See the discussion of Peyronie's disease at Aetna Intelihealth, an Internet resource reviewed by the faculty of the Harvard Medical School: http://www.intelihealth.com/IH/ihtIH/WSIHW000/9339/10519.html.

24. See Mace, *Sexual Difficulties in Marriage*, 22–32.

25. See "Aging alone . . . does not abolish sexual desire or functioning" (175). Gary J. Kennedy, M.D., *Geriatric Mental Health Care: A Treatment Guide for Health Professionals* (New York: Guilford Press, 2000), chap. 9, "Sexuality," 175–91.

26. See Sandra R. Leiblum and Raymond C. Rosen, "Introduction: Sex Therapy in the Age of Viagra," in *Principles and Practice of Sex Therapy*, 3rd ed., edited by Sandra R. Leiblum and Raymond C. Rosen (New York: Guilford Press, 2000), 3–12.

27. Male clergy are referred to Rassieur, *Problem Clergymen Don't Talk About*.
28. "In developing definitions of terms related to our policy recommendations, the Task Force relies on and in this section quotes from materials developed by the Center for the Prevention of Sexual and Domestic Violence (CPSDV) in Seattle, Washington.

    Domestic violence is a pattern of assaultive and coercive behavior, including physical, sexual, and psychological attacks as well as economic coercion, that adults or adolescents use against their intimate partners or vulnerable family members. In abusive relationships, perpetrators use their power in ways that inflict harm on others for the perpetrators' own need for power and control.

    Violence can take many forms. Among the most common are physical, emotional (also known as psychological maltreatment), sexual, and neglectful. Physical abuse is the use of brute force, such as hitting, biting, kicking, slapping, burning or scalding, to damage a person's body. The weapon may be a fist, a knife, a gun, or other object. Physical abuse generally involves willful acts by a perpetrator, resulting in injury to the victim; however, it may also result when the perpetrator's intent is not to injure or harm the victim, as in corporal punishment." Office of the General Assembly, "Turn Mourning into Dancing!" 20.
29. See Douglas Larsen, "The Domestic Violence Cycle," who states, "Most programs for batterers have only about a 5% success rate" at http://incestabuse.about.com/od/domesticabuse/a/dvcycle_2.htm.
30. Daniel Jay Sonkin, Del Martin, and Lenore E. A. Walker, *The Male Batterer: A Treatment Approach* (New York: Springer Publishing Co., 1985), 2.
31. Nason-Clark, *Battered Wife*, 7. See also Adams, *Woman-Battering*; and Clarke, *Pastoral Care of Battered Women*.
32. Vicky Whipple, "Counseling Battered Women from Fundamentalist Churches," *Journal of Marital and Family Therapy* 13, no. 3 (July 1987): 251.
33. The term "victim" has its limitations, particularly in its connotation of complete helplessness. Actually, most victims of domestic violence are not helpless when they come to realize the power they have in making better choices to protect themselves and their children.
34. See "XIV. A Pastoral Response to Domestic Violence," in Office of the General Assembly, "Turn Mourning into Dancing!" 31–32.
35. See Howard Clinebell's discussion of the EISPUA categories of counselor responses in *Basic Types of Pastoral Care and Counseling*, 94–96.
36. Adams, *Woman-Battering*, 68.
37. Douglas J. Wiebe, "Homicide and Suicide Risks Associated with Firearms in the Home: A National Case-Control Study," *Annals of Emergency Medicine* 41, no. 6 (June 2003): 771–82.
38. I once had the shocking experience of seeing a report on the local news of the shooting deaths of a husband and wife who were at the time coming to me for marriage counseling. The husband first killed his wife and then turned the gun on himself.
39. See http://endabuse.org/resources/gethelp.
40. See Larsen, "The Domestic Violence Cycle" at http://incestabuse.about.com/od/domesticabuse/a/dvcycle.htm.
41. Adams, *Woman-Battering*, 57–59.
42. See Culbertson, "Divorce Counseling," in *Caring for God's People*, 159–89, and Switzer, *Pastoral Care Emergencies*, 146–58.

43. See William B. Oglesby, Jr., "Divorce and Remarriage in Christian Perspective," *Pastoral Psychology* 25, no. 4 (Summer 1977): 282–93. See also Abigail Rian Evans, "Dissolution of Partnerships/Marriage," in *Healing Liturgies for the Seasons of Life* (Louisville, KY: Westminster John Knox Press, 2004), 110–18.

44. See Emerick-Cayton, *Divorcing with Dignity Mediation*. Other alternative dispute resolution resources include the American Arbitration Association: (http://www.adr.org/index2.1.jsp), and MediationNow.com (http://www.mediationnow.com/communal/links.htm). In addition, collaborative law is practiced by many attorneys and seeks to avoid litigation and court involvement. See, for example, the Web site for the Collaborative Law Alliance of New Hampshire (http://www.collaborativelawnh.org).

45. David and Vera Mace, *In the Presence of God: Readings for Christian Marriage* (Philadelphia: Westminster Press, 1985), 45.

46. Stewart, *Minister as Marriage Counselor* (1961 ed.), 7.

Appendix D

1. See Abigail Rian Evans, "Dissolution of Partnerships/Marriage," in *Healing Liturgies for the Seasons of Life* (Louisville, KY: Westminster John Knox Press, 2004), 110–18.

Bibliography

Reading by itself cannot be a substitute for the professional supervision or peer review of one's counseling. But parish pastors can enlarge their perspective on marriage and marriage counseling by reading books in this limited, core bibliography. Books not referenced in the notes have been marked with an asterisk.

Adams, Carol J. *Woman-Battering*. Minneapolis: Fortress Press, 1994.

*Anderson, Herbert, Don S. Browning, Ian S. Evison, and Mary Stewart Van Leeuwen, eds. *The Family Handbook*. Louisville, KY: Westminster John Knox Press, 1998.

*———, David Hogue, and Marie McCarthy. *Promising Again*. Louisville, KY: Westminster John Knox Press, 1995.

*———, and Susan B. W. Johnson. *Regarding Children: A New Respect for Childhood and Families*. Louisville, KY: Westminster John Knox Press, 1994.

*Apthorp, Stephen P. *Alcohol and Substance Abuse: A Handbook for Clergy and Congregations*. 2nd ed. New York: Authors Choice Press, 2003.

Augsburger, David W. *Pastoral Counseling across Cultures*. Philadelphia: Westminster Press, 1986.

*Bach, George R., with Peter Wyden. *The Intimate Enemy: How to Fight Fair in Love and Marriage*. New York: Avon Books, 1981.

*Berne, Eric. *Games People Play: The Psychology of Human Relationships*. 40th anniversary ed. New York: Ballantine Books, 2004.

Buber, Martin. *Between Man and Man*. Translated by Ronald G. Smith and Maurice Friedman. New York: Macmillan Company, 1965.

———. *I and Thou*. Translated by Ronald G. Smith. Edinburgh: T. & T. Clark, 1937.

Capps, Donald. *Giving Counsel: A Minister's Guidebook*. St. Louis: Chalice Press, 2001.

Carnes, Patrick. *Contrary to Love: Helping the Sexual Addict*. Center City, MN: Hazelden Foundation, 1994. First published 1989 by CompCare Publishers.

———. *Out of the Shadows: Understanding Sexual Addiction*. 3rd ed. Center City, MN: Hazelden Publishing and Educational Services, 2001.

———, David L. Delmonico, and Elizabeth Griffin, with Joseph M. Moriarity. *In the*

Shadows of the Net: Breaking Free of Compulsive Online Sexual Behavior. Center City, MN: Hazelden, 2001.

Clarke, Rita-Lou. *Pastoral Care of Battered Women*. Philadelphia: Westminster Press, 1986.

*Clinebell, Charlotte H. *Meet Me in the Middle: On Becoming Human Together*. New York: Harper & Row, 1973.

Clinebell, Howard J. *Basic Types of Pastoral Care and Counseling: Resources for the Ministry of Healing and Growth*. Rev. ed. Nashville: Abingdon Press, 1984.

———. *Basic Types of Pastoral Counseling: New Resources for Ministering to the Troubled*. Nashville: Abingdon Press, 1966.

*———. *Growth Counseling for Marriage Enrichment: Pre-Marriage and the Early Years*. Philadelphia: Fortress Press, 1975.

*———. *Growth Counseling for Mid-Years Couples*. Philadelphia: Fortress Press, 1977.

———, and Charlotte H. Clinebell. *The Intimate Marriage*. New York: Harper & Row, 1970.

Culbertson, Philip. *Caring for God's People: Counseling and Christian Wholeness*. Minneapolis: Fortress Press, 2000.

Dittes, James E. *Pastoral Counseling: The Basics*. Louisville, KY: Westminster John Knox Press, 1999.

Emerick-Cayton, Tim. *Divorcing with Dignity Mediation: The Sensible Alternative*. Louisville, KY: Westminster/John Knox Press, 1993.

*Evans, Abigail Rian. *Healing Liturgies for the Seasons of Life*. Louisville, KY: Westminster John Knox Press, 2004.

*Fortune, Marie M. *Is Nothing Sacred? When Sex Invades the Pastoral Relationship*. San Francisco: Harper & Row, 1989.

Garland, Diana S. Richmond, and David E. Garland. *Beyond Companionship: Christians in Marriage*. Philadelphia: Westminster Press, 1986.

*Gilbert, Maria, and Diana Shmukler. *Brief Therapy with Couples: An Integrative Approach*. New York: John Wiley & Sons, 1996.

Griffin, Benjamin T. "Children Whose Parents Are Divorcing." Pages 69–81 in *When Children Suffer: A Sourcebook for Ministry with Children in Crisis*, edited by Andrew D. Lester. Philadelphia: Westminster Press, 1987.

*Grossoehme, Daniel H. *The Pastoral Care of Children*. New York: Haworth Pastoral Press, 1999.

Hendrix, Harville. *Getting the Love You Want: A Guide for Couples*. New York: Henry Holt & Co., 1988.

Howe, Reuel L. *The Miracle of Dialogue*. Greenwich, CT: Seabury Press, 1963.

*Jackson, Nicky Ali, and Giselé Casanova Oates, eds. *Violence in Intimate Relationships: Examining Sociological and Psychological Issues*. Boston: Butterworth-Heinemann, 1998.

Jay, Jeff, and Debra Jay. *Love First: A New Approach to Intervention for Alcoholism and Drug Addiction*. Center City, MN: Hazelden, 2000.

*Karpel, Mark A. *Evaluating Couples: A Handbook for Practitioners*. New York: W. W. Norton & Co., 1994.

*Keller, John E. *Ministering to Alcoholics*. Rev. ed. Minneapolis: Augsburg, 1991.

Lebacqs, Karen, and Ronald G. Barton. *Sex in the Parish*. Louisville, KY: Westminster/John Knox Press, 1991.

———, and Joseph D. Driskill. *Ethics and Spiritual Care: A Guide for Pastors, Chaplains, and Spiritual Directors*. Nashville: Abingdon Press, 2000.

*Lederer, William J., and Don D. Jackson. *The Mirages of Marriage*. New York: W. W. Norton & Co., 1968.

Lester, Andrew D. *Hope in Pastoral Care and Counseling*. Louisville, KY: Westminster John Knox Press, 1995.

———. *Pastoral Care with Children in Crisis*. Philadelphia: Westminster Press, 1985.

———, ed. *When Children Suffer: A Sourcebook for Ministry with Children in Crisis*. Philadelphia: Westminster Press, 1987.

*———, and Judith L. Lester. *It Takes Two: The Joy of Intimate Marriage*. Louisville, KY: Westminster John Knox Press, 1998.

Masters, William H., Virginia E. Johnson, and Robert C. Kolodny. *Masters and Johnson on Sex and Human Loving*. Boston: Little, Brown & Co., 1986.

*McGoldrick, Monica, and Randy Gerson. *Genograms in Family Assessment*. New York: W. W. Norton & Co., 1985.

*Miles, Rebekah L. *The Pastor as Moral Guide*. Minneapolis: Fortress Press, 1999.

*Miller, Sherod, Daniel Wackman, Elam Nunnally, and Carol Saline. *Straight Talk: A New Way to Get Closer to Others by Saying What You Really Mean*. New York: Rawson, Wade Publishers, 1981.

Nason-Clark, Nancy. *The Battered Wife: How Christians Confront Family Violence*. Louisville, KY: Westminster John Knox Press, 1997.

*Neuger, Christie Cozad. *Counseling Women: A Narrative, Pastoral Approach*. Minneapolis: Fortress Press, 2001.

Oates, Wayne E. *The Christian Pastor*. 3rd ed. Philadelphia: Westminster Press, 1982.

Office of the General Assembly, "Turn Mourning into Dancing! A Policy Statement on Healing Domestic Violence and Study Guide." Louisville, KY: Office of the General Assembly, Presbyterian Church (U.S.A.), 2001. May be viewed at http://www.pcusa.org/oga/publications/dancing.pdf.

*Oglesby, William B., Jr. *Referral in Pastoral Counseling*. Rev. ed. Nashville: Abingdon Press, 1978.

Ragsdale, Katherine Hancock, ed. *Boundary Wars: Intimacy and Distance in Healing Relationships*. Cleveland: Pilgrim Press, 1996.

Rassieur, Charles L. *The Problem Clergymen Don't Talk About*. Philadelphia: Westminster Press, 1976.

*Rediger, G. Lloyd. *Beyond the Scandals: A Guide to Healthy Sexuality for Clergy*. Minneapolis: Fortress Press, 2003.

*Rubin, Lillian B. *Intimate Strangers: Men and Women Together*. New York: Harper & Row, 1983.

Rutter, Peter. *Sex in the Forbidden Zone: When Men in Power—Therapists, Doctors, Clergy, Teachers, and Others—Betray Women's Trust*. New York: Fawcett Crest, 1989.

Sager, Clifford J. *Marriage Contracts and Couple Therapy: Hidden Forces in Intimate Relationships*. New York: Brunner/Mazel, 1976.

*Schaef, Anne Wilson. *Co-Dependence: Misunderstood-Mistreated*. San Francisco: HarperCollins, 1992.

*Shelp, Earl E., and Ronald H. Sunderland. *AIDS and the Church: The Second Decade*. Rev. ed. Louisville, KY: Westminster/John Knox Press, 1992.

Stewart, Charles William. *The Minister as Marriage Counselor*. 1961. Reprint, Nashville: Abingdon Press, 1970.

Stone, Howard W. *Brief Pastoral Counseling: Short-Term Approaches and Strategies*. Minneapolis: Fortress Press, 1994.

*———. *Crisis Counseling*. Rev. ed. Minneapolis: Fortress Press, 1993.

———, ed. *Strategies for Brief Pastoral Counseling*. Minneapolis: Fortress Press, 2001.

———, and William M. Clements, eds. *Handbook for Basic Types of Pastoral Care and Counseling*. Nashville: Abingdon Press, 1991.

*Sunderland, Ronald H., and Earl E. Shelp. *AIDS, A Manual for Pastoral Care*. Philadelphia: Westminster Press, 1987.

Switzer, David K. *The Minister as Crisis Counselor*. Rev. ed. Nashville: Abingdon Press, 1986.

———. *Pastoral Care Emergencies*. Minneapolis: Fortress Press, 2000.

*Tannen, Deborah. *You Just Don't Understand: Women and Men in Conversation*. New York: Ballantine Books, 1990.

Tillich, Paul. *Systematic Theology*. Vol. 1. Chicago: University of Chicago Press, 1951.

Tournier, Paul. *To Understand Each Other*. Translated by John S. Gilmour. Richmond: John Knox Press, 1967.

*Trull, Joe E., and James E. Carter. *Ministerial Ethics: Being a Good Minister in a Not-So-Good World*. Nashville: Broadman & Holman, 1993.

*Visher, Emily B., and John S. Visher. *Stepfamilies: A Guide to Working with Stepparents and Stepchildren*. New York: Brunner/Mazel, 1979.

Wallerstein, Judith S., and Sandra Blakeslee. *The Good Marriage: How and Why Love Lasts*. Boston: Houghton Mifflin, 1995.

———, Julia Lewis, and Sandra Blakeslee. *The Unexpected Legacy of Divorce: A 25 Year Landmark Study*. New York: Hyperion, 2000.

*Weaver, Andrew J., and Carolyn L. Stapleton, eds. *Reflections on Marriage and Spiritual Growth*. Nashville: Abingdon Press, 2003.

Wegscheider-Cruse, Sharon. *Another Chance: Hope and Health for the Alcoholic Family*. 2nd ed. Palo Alto, CA: Science & Behavior Books, 1989.

*Weiner-Davis, Michele. *Divorce Busting: A Revolutionary and Rapid Program for Staying Together*. New York: Summit Books, 1992.

*West, James W. *The Betty Ford Center Book of Answers: Help for Those Struggling with Substance Abuse and for the People Who Love Them*. New York: Pocket Books, 1997.

Wiest, Walter E., and Elwyn A. Smith. *Ethics in Ministry: A Guide for the Professional*. Minneapolis: Fortress Press, 1990.

Woititz, Janet Geringer. *Adult Children of Alcoholics*. Expanded ed. Deerfield Beach, FL: Health Communications, 1990.

Pastors are also encouraged to refer to the following journals:

Family Ministry: Empowering Through Faith

Family Relations: Interdisciplinary Journal of Applied Family Studies

Journal of Family Issues

Journal of Marital and Family Therapy

Journal of Marriage and Family

Journal of Ministry in Addiction and Recovery

Journal of Sex and Marital Therapy

Pastoral Psychology

The Journal of Pastoral Care and Counseling